FAMOUS HISTORICAL MYSTERIES

The famous mysteries related in this book include some that have offered a challenge to many generations of readers. That challenge remains just as tantalizing today, for most of these mysteries still await a final and conclusive solution.

Here the author not only gives the known facts, but presents them in a dramatic narrative that makes a gripping adventure story of each episode. The reader can thus accept the challenge others have taken up before him, and try his own skill at solving one of the great and enduring mysteries of all time.

LEONARD GRIBBLE

Famous Historical Mysteries

FREDERICK MULLER

*First published in Great Britain in 1969
by Frederick Muller Limited, Fleet Street, London E.C.4*

Copyright © 1969 Leonard Gribble

*Printed and bound in Great Britain by
The Garden City Press Limited
Letchworth, Hertfordshire*

SBN: 584 62015 2

Contents

Contents

Introduction

One of the most intriguing, as well as the most human, facets of history is the challenge of those mysteries that have never been entirely solved to the satisfaction of all who study them.

Some of these mysteries have a touch of the bizarre, others of the macabre, while quite a few have that natural pathos that only a story taken from real life can provide its readers.

Here are ten such time-wrapped mysteries of the past, involving people whose personal destinies sometimes helped to shape wider events than their own lives. Others concern individuals whose actions seem to demand a broader explanation that what is guaranteed by the known facts.

The ten mysteries cover many centuries and have been selected not only for the inherent challenge each holds, but for their wide diversity of interesting human drama and the vastly different and contrasting pictures they provide of other times. They reveal cruelty because sometimes they picture less civilized eras of the broad human story, but they also contain redeeming glimpses of the human spirit accepting with fortitude the grimly inevitable. This is not the least of their challenges to the reader.

The subjects included reveal the actions of both strong men and weak, but they also emphasize the curious fact that often the destinies of mere children have provided problems in high policy that have resulted in some of the most dramatic of all historical mysteries.

Naturally account has to be taken of both rumour and legend, for sometimes it is with such warp and woof that the historical mystery is woven to its most intriguing limits. Moreover, some rumours circulate only because a person has obtained knowledge thought to be secret, while legends often focus a folk belief that makes its own demands on our credibilities and even our feelings.

To ensure that these mysteries provided by the past centuries are as widely representative as possible, a mystery of the sea has been included. Of its kind, it is as challenging as the real identity of a masked prisoner of State or the mystery surrounding the end of a king who gambled his life and kingdom on one bold throw to alter the course of history – and lost.

There is likewise a mystery provided by an incredible court case involving persons from all parts of the world, which is without parallel, and another human drama that demonstrates how the passionate attachment of one person for another can produce circumstances both tragic and shrouded in mystery.

Because their inherent drama is so compelling, a number of the mysteries included here have been incorporated into novels by writers seeking a subject that offers a richer strangeness than invented fiction. But here, in each case, the story offered is limited to the evidence of history, and the reader is afforded an opportunity to supply a purely personal explanation to some dubious events that the past has presented as unique dramas with a perpetual challenge.

The Mystery of Kaspar Hauser

For nearly a century and a half the mystery of this apparently inarticulate youth, who suddenly appeared out of nowhere in the middle of a populous German city, has teased the minds and imaginations of historians, novelists, and playwrights.

It was on a bright Whit-Monday afternoon in May 1828, when the townsfolk of Nuremberg were abroad in the streets on holiday, that a patrolling policeman saw a crowd of youngsters gesticulating and shouting at someone in their midst. The thickset Bavarian guardian of the local law strolled across to the noisy group of youths to see what had attracted their attention and given rise to their catcalls and taunting shouts. He found them gathered in a wide circle around a bewildered youth of about sixteen who was trying without much success to speak.

The youth stuttered and stammered, but no intelligible words issued from his moving lips, and there was a scared look on his face. His hair was unkempt and his clothes, which appeared home-made and very unlike the coats and trousers of the Nuremberg lads who were taunting him, were bedraggled and shapeless. When his tormentors saw the approaching policeman they ran off, releasing a fresh stream of unkind catcalls.

The frowning policeman stopped a short distance from the strange youth and ran a disapproving eye over his curious garb.

"What's your name and where are you from?" the policeman asked.

Aware that he was being spoken to, the youth made a show of replying, but, as before, only inarticulate sounds came from his mouth.

"Speak up and speak clearly," the policeman ordered sharply.

Perhaps it was the sharp tone that frightened the strange youth. He suddenly threw up his arms and cowered back, as though protecting his head from expected blows. The policeman stared in disbelief as the youth stooped with a quick ducking motion of his body and picked up the hat that had been knocked from his head by his tormentors. The hat was crammed down on his unkempt hair.

It was a felt hat, round and high in the crown, and in the quick glimpse he had received of its inside the policeman had noticed that it was lined with what appeared to be red leather and yellow silk. He had seen many hats, but not one like this strange youth's.

The policeman's glance dropped to the youngster's feet. They were encased in a pair of cracked and scuffed morocco leather shoes of great age. Moreover, they had such high heels, rather like a woman's shoes, that the curious youth pitched badly when he walked, as though he was not used to the feel of them cramping his feet. There was a grubby black silk handkerchief around the skinny throat that was producing a string of unintelligible sounds, and the youth's body and legs were covered by a grey cloth jacket and worn riding-breeches.

It was quite a scarecrow to find on a May afternoon in the centre of Nuremberg.

"You'd better come along with me," the policeman decided.

Seizing the frightened youth's arm, he turned back the way he had come and arrived at the police station with a crowd of interested sightseers trailing behind.

With the doors closed on the small crowd in the street, the spluttering and scared youth was asked a number of questions by various police officials. To every question he replied with the same unintelligible sounds.

It looked as though Nuremberg had been visited by someone who had never learned to talk!

The youth's clothes were taken from him and examined in the hope of providing a clue to his identity. The policeman, running his hand over the lining of the grey jacket, found more than just a clue. He came upon a letter that had been carefully stitched inside the grey cloth.

The letter appeared to be written in a sloping feminine hand. It was dated sixteen years previously, and was addressed to anyone who found "the baby". The finder was exhorted to take care of a child that had been discarded. The writer, presumably the child's mother, gave some guarded information when she wrote :

"I am a poor girl and cannot look after my child. His name is Kaspar Hauser. He has already been baptized. His father is dead. He was a soldier. When he is sixteen years old I beg of you to send him to Nuremberg, to the Sixth Cavalry Regiment. His father used to belong to it."

The writer had not signed her name. However, her letter proved to be a startling document. As the chief of police pointed out when he was shown the letter, it would not have been possible for anyone writing sixteen years earlier to have known that the Sixth Cavalry Regiment would have been stationed in Nuremberg at that time.

That particular regiment had been in Nuremberg until only a few days before, when it had been ordered to leave at very short notice and quite unexpectedly.

"The letter's a forgery," the chief of the Nuremberg police declared. "This is borne out by the ink. It is not at all faded, as it would be after sixteen years."

Which was a very shrewd point. But there was a complication. A second letter was found stitched into the clothes of the speechless youth. It appeared to be in a different hand, and its writer claimed to be a labourer, who stated that the boy had been given into his charge on October 7th, 1812. As the first letter claimed the boy Kaspar had been born on April 30 that year, he had been a little over five months old when the writer of the second letter became his guardian. The latter went on to explain that he had agreed to have the boy taught how to read and write, and had seen that he had been brought up a Christian, but admitted that the child had been kept in what was described as close confinement.

In short, if the letters were to be taken at face value, Kaspar

Hauser was an unwanted child who had been brought up by a stranger and kept away from all normal human contacts.

Why?

The youth himself either could not or would not answer any of the fresh questions directed at him. He remained in the police station at Nuremberg, a terrible problem child for the local police to handle.

"We can't keep him unless he's charged," the police chief pointed out to his assistants. "So he'd better be charged as a vagrant. That will give us a chance to find out more about him."

So the youth, with some golden down on his cheek to support the claim that he was sixteen, was taken from the police station and lodged in the Vestner Tower. As soon as his cell door clanged shut on him, the youth now known as Kaspar Hauser flung himself upon the straw bed provided by the Nuremberg authorities for the nightly comfort of vagrants and vagabonds, and without appearing in the slightest way concerned by his reception and treatment in the Bavarian city, closed his eyes, turned to face the wall, and within minutes was sleeping soundly.

He awoke to find the authorities had been in conference about the new arrival in the city. After he had been fed Kaspar was taken to be medically examined by a doctor with a stern face and repellent whiskers. More questions were shouted at him. He cringed. Questions were whispered at him, whereupon he looked bemused. His body reflexes were tested. Tricks were played upon him, to take him by surprise. The process wore away most of a morning. At the end of these persevering hours the doctor pronounced his finding.

Kaspar Hauser was no more than a child in intelligence, although he was approaching puberty and his physical development fully supported the claim that he was between sixteen and seventeen years old. However, the Nuremberg doctor sensed that he had to provide some eyebrow-raising comment, so he added to his findings as a medical man his personal opinion that there must be a profound mystery at the root of this unnatural and retarded development.

After the jail mire had been cleansed from Kaspar's flesh with the other filth it had acquired, it was observed that his skin was fair and of a soft texture, unlike the skin of a working man's child. He had slender arms and legs, but they were well formed and proportioned. The boy's feet were small for his age, but their soles were as soft as the flesh of a small child. When encouraged to walk alone he was seen to stumble, somewhat in the manner of a child who has only very recently mastered how to maintain balance when putting one foot in front of the other. When a chair was put in his path he did not turn aside from it, but continued to collide with it, and then he stumbled and more often than not could not recover his lost balance, and fell down. When he fell he whimpered like a small child. It was found that he had almost no sense of how to use or employ his fingers. He held them stiffly out in front of him, and when induced to grasp and retain an object he used the flat of his entire hand. Although he appeared to have normal vision, his eyes retained a vacant expression for long periods, as though his immediate surroundings held little of interest for him. In repose his facial expression was heavy, almost sullen, but when he was pleased a quick smile transformed his features, lending them a brief look of pleasant awareness.

The Nuremberg authorities transferred him to a special room, where he was observed like a specimen in a laboratory, and indeed that was really what he was, for the only way to communicate with him during the first weeks after his sudden and unexplained appearance in the city was by signs. After he had come to recognize certain signs for what they were intended to convey, an effort was made to help him master articulate speech. Once his interest was captured he learned with growing ease.

However, if his tongue had been left untutored for far too long, there was nothing subnormal about his memory, which was both retentive and adaptive in conveying what it had retained. As his vocabulary grew so did the urge to tell what was stored in his mind. Little by little he imparted a story that was both incredible and utterly unique. He informed those who sought to unlock his store of personal history that he had lived all his life in a dark place underground, rather like a dungeon or a hermit's cell. He did not speak with the man who came to bring him food, and who was virtually his jailer. The boy explained that he had not been ill-treated, and had not been made to work or suffer privation of any kind. He had been well fed, but the only toys he remembered playing with were made of wood, simple things constructed for a very young child. He had also been given a crudely carved wooden horse.

He had lived, for the most part, unbathed and even unwashed. He had been washed only at rare intervals which he had no way of measuring. The man who had brought him his food and drink had appeared twice during each day.

It was a stark, terribly simple story that did not take long to tell. But when his questioners again arrived at the problem of how he had come to appear in the streets of Nuremberg, they saw the former scared look return to his face, and he stood quivering and trembling in front of them.

While he had no constructive idea of where he had been kept during his solitary life underground, he had sharp impressions of the recent change in his living conditions. He had been forced to leave the place where he had been imprisoned for so long, and upon finding himself compelled to walk had discovered that he had very little sense of balance and putting one foot in front of the other had been a great effort requiring considerable concentration. When told to hurry he had fallen down.

He had been beaten for his clumsiness.

Indeed, he had only been able to totter as far as a forest before falling down exhausted. The grim-faced man accompanying him had given him a kick and hurried away. Some time later he returned driving a closed carriage. Kaspar had been helped inside and the door closed on him. It had been hot and he had been thirsty.

The carriage's wheels seemed to the youth to be rolling and bumping along for hours before the driver called to the horse and the swaying motion ceased.

The door had opened and he had been forced outside. While he stood looking in wonder at the sight of nearby houses the carriage had been driven away. Kaspar Hauser was alone in a world where he was a complete stranger.

He began stumbling towards the paved streets of Nuremberg, lost, bewildered, unable to communicate with those who approached him to stare in astonishment at this apparition that had arrived from nowhere.

That was his incredible story, drawn from him by painful process of constant inquiry. It was a story that captured the imagination not only of Germans, but of people in other European countries. Even the Nuremberg police chief, who had condemned the letter from the writer purporting to be the youth's mother as a forgery, was forced to admit that there must be more than just an element of truth in the fantastic story of a child brought up like an animal, away from human contact, so that he approached manhood with the intelligence of an infant.

It was the police chief who started the inquiry that was to end by the creation of a legend more incredible and fantastic than the halting story produced by the slow-tongued Kaspar Hauser. He had inquiries made throughout Bavaria to try to find the person or persons responsible for the child's imprisonment. The officials making the inquiries were approached by a fisherman who produced a bottle he had found two years before. Inside was a third letter. It was signed by a certain Hares Sprauka.

The writer claimed to be living a kind of Monte Cristo existence, kept in a subterranean cell in a fortress prison near Lauffenburg, on the Rhine.

The letter had no significance until one of the police inquirers started puzzling over that most unlikely signature. He found that, by transposing the letters, he had the name Kaspar Hauser!

Yet obviously it could not have been written by the mystery

youth of Nuremberg. Further inquiries were directed to Lauffenburg. Their outcome has never been made known, but it was not long after this that an attempt was made to assassinate the youth being held by the police in Nuremberg. Apparently someone was anxious that interest in his existence and past story should cease.

The would-be assassin was masked, and he broke into the room where Kaspar was sleeping and hurriedly stabbed him. The blade entered the youth's left breast. Fortunately the intruder was in a hurry, and although the stab wound resulted in a dragging illness it did not prove fatal. When the youth could be safely moved he was taken to Anspach.

By this time interest in the mysterious Kaspar Hauser was extending throughout Europe, and one Professor Daumer came forward and offered his assistance in educating and rehabilitating the backward adolescent. An English nobleman, the Earl of Stanhope, also became interested in the fabulous story that was growing like a legend. His daughter Catherine, who later became the Duchess of Cleveland and mother of Lord Rosebery, joined her father in his desire to unravel the mystery of Kaspar Hauser. Father and daughter helped the youth in Anspach and when he was twenty secured his employment in the office of a notary named Feuerbach, and it was in this year, 1832, that research and further inquiry resulted in shaping a story about the youth's origins that still persists.

A group of fervent researchers claimed that Kaspar Hauser was no less than the legitimate Crown Prince of Baden.

It was in the year 1812 that the infant Crown Prince vanished from the Palace of Karlsruhe on a night of wild storm, with a great wind whistling and moaning among the castle turrets. On that night one of the servants claimed he saw the White Lady in one of the many corridors. The White Lady was a ghost whose appearance was associated with an imminent death in the royal family of Baden. However, the avid seekers after the true origin of Kaspar Hauser decided that the veiled figure seen that stormy night in Karlsruhe was no ghost, despite the servant's claim that the nocturnal visitor had passed through a wall.

The person mistaken for the legendary White Lady was a woman hurrying to a secret sliding panel concealed by wall tapestries. Beyond the panel was the nursery where the infant Crown Prince slept, with two snoring nurses for night guard. The nurses, it was later claimed, had been drugged and knew nothing of the female intruder who lifted the baby from his silver cradle and substituted, in his stead, another infant that had been smuggled into the palace.

The exchanged babies were similar in age and sex. But whereas the one taken from the silver cradle was fresh-complexioned and healthy, the changeling left to supplant him was very pale and had ceased breathing. In short, a dead child had replaced the living infant taken from the Crown Prince's nursery.

A few hours later the Grand-Duchess Stephanie was bewailing the death of her small son. She had been told he had died suddenly and unexpectedly during that night of storm and great winds. The loss left her inconsolable, for she now believed that the heir to the throne of Baden would be not her own child, but the child of a woman she hated, the Countess von Hochberg, who had contracted a morganatic marriage with the prince, Karl Frederick.

After the lapse of twenty years the speedy funeral of the supposed son of the Grand-Duchess Stephanie appeared to have been undertaken with what seemed to be undue haste. The mourning mother, it was said, had not been allowed to take a last glimpse of the dead child in its elaborate coffin. The reason given was that the infant had died of a malady that was contagious.

It was sometime after the funeral that the Grand-Duchess heard of the servant who had seen the ghost of the White Lady on the night her son had died.

She sent for the man.

"Tell me precisely what you saw that night," she ordered.

In faltering tones the man told of seeing the cloaked female who appeared to vanish through a wall. The Grand-Duchess became convinced that she and her son had been the victims of a cruel intrigue.

If she had any doubts they were resolved when, a few days later, the servant who had told her of seeing the White Lady was found dead in his bed. The personal physician of Karl Frederick examined the corpse.

"Death was due to apoplexy," he announced.

After that announcement there was no further inquiry at the time into the cause of the servant's death. But the Grand-Duchess, who knew very well how much the physician was the obedient hireling of Karl Frederick, was convinced that the man she had questioned had been poisoned.

She could do nothing save grieve, for to make any overt move against the interests of the Countess von Hochberg, she knew, might mean a still greater disaster overtaking her.

But while the Grand-Duchess Stephanie remained a virtual prisoner in her own quarters of the palace, rumours began to circulate beyond its walls.

Those inquirers of a score of years later learned of the wife of a palace worker who lived a short distance from the walls. On the night the little Crown Prince was supposed to have died of a contagious disease, she told some friends and neighbours, she had sat up late suffering from toothache. It was very late that night when she heard the wheels of a carriage approaching over the cobblestones. Between howling gusts of wind she heard the carriage come to a stop, and she had looked out of a window and seen it drawn up before a small postern gate in the wall.

The woman, for a few moments, forgot the pain under her tooth as she stared with wide eyes at sight of a female figure getting down from the carriage and carrying a well-wrapped bundle in her arms. The woman alighting from the carriage was closely veiled so that her face could not be seen and she would not be recognized. The carriage remained by the postern gate until the woman reappeared, still carrying a bundle. She had entered the carriage, and as soon as the door was closed upon her the coachman drove off.

To the later inquirers it seemed that these rumours had died suddenly, almost as though killed by fear.

It was not difficult for such interested persons as Professor Daumer and the notary Feuerbach to evolve a theory about what had happened that grim night of 1812 and associate events with the mysterious Kaspar Hauser.

To them it seemed that this youth was, in truth, the son and legitimate heir of the Grand-Duke Karl Frederick of Baden. The infant Crown Prince had been kidnapped from his nursery in Karlsruhe on that night twenty years before in October 1812, and the plot had been contrived and carried out by friends of the Countess von Hochberg, who wished her own son to supplant the legitimate heir.

When the new-found friends of the young man of twenty known as Kaspar Hauser sought to unravel the mystery further, they suddenly found themselves confronted by a wall of silence. Officials who might have been expected to produce facts and records were suddenly either unwilling or unable to oblige. It was said that some of the persons making the inquiries were threatened with violence if they did not desist. However, the Earl of Stanhope, who had accepted fully the theory for which Professor Daumer was mainly responsible, was convinced that despite the failure of the authorities to find who had kept Kaspar Hauser imprisoned for more than sixteen years, and whereabouts they had done so before releasing him in Nuremberg, the Grand-Duchess Stephanie should be told the truth.

He wrote to her a very detailed letter and asked her to come to Anspach, where she could be reunited with her son.

However, the dispatch of that letter served as the death knell for the young man whose origin had become a topic of debate in salons throughout Europe where the liberal-minded foregathered. The Grand-Duchess received the letter and was overjoyed at the promise it held. The thought of meeting her son again after so many lost years seemed to blind her to the possibility that there could be a mistake. The letter was written with such obvious sincerity that she had no doubt that this young man, Kaspar Hauser, working as an articled clerk in a notary's office in Anspach, was the son she had so long mourned as dead.

She made arrangements to visit Anspach as soon as she could.

Unfortunately her speed was of no avail, and the woman who had once had her hopes crushed was doomed to a second brutal disappointment. She was not to see Kaspar Hauser and claim him as her son.

He died before she could reach the Bavarian town that was about thirty miles from Nuremberg, and his death was as mysterious as any facet of his curious life.

While the Grand-Duchess was actually en route to meet him, Kaspar left his lodgings in Anspach and went for a walk in a public park. It was a cold morning in December 1833, and the shrubs and blades of grass were coated with frost. Kaspar had told no one he was going to the park.

His reason for going there remained a secret until after his body had been found.

He had received earlier a letter from someone who claimed to be able to clear up, finally and without leaving any room for doubt, the riddle of his past and of his rightful identity. He was asked to keep a secret rendezvous in the park.

It seemed at last as if Kaspar Hauser, who had been struggling for the past five years to fit himself into a world that had burst upon him with shattering effect one day when he was sixteen, would be able to find out for himself who he was.

Whom he met on his lonely walk in the park is not known.

But later his body was found on the frozen ground. Blood soaked his shirt-front and his coat. He had been stabbed with a slim blade like that of a stiletto. He was barely breathing when found.

While physicians tried in vain to save his life he muttered in his broken, hesitant fashion of a stranger who had come up to him and suddenly attacked him. By the time the Grand-Duchess

Stephanie's coach was rumbling through the streets of the Bavarian town, Kaspar Hauser was dead.

The date was December 14th, 1833, just ten days before Christmas.

With the strange young man's death local interest died, but the legend grew. It took strength from the fact that in the dying Kaspar Hauser's pocket was found the letter which directed his steps that morning to the park where he received the fatal wound.

The Earl of Stanhope, shocked by his protégé's violent death, offered what was then an enormous reward, a thousand pounds, for the capture and conviction of the murderer. But no one came forward with information that resulted in the killer's arrest. The Grand-Duchess Stephanie devoted years to trying to discover who had brought about the death of the young man she was convinced was her lost son. Her efforts proved useless, but they served, in their turn, to lend substance to the growing legend of Kaspar Hauser.

It was not until more than forty years later, in 1875, that the Augsburg *Allgemeine Zeitung* published what was claimed to be the official record of the baptism, post-mortem, and burial of the young heir to Grand-Duke Karl Frederick, the infant son of the Grand-Duchess Stephanie. A year later the mystery was dealt with in a volume published in Heidelberg, and this proved to be source material for two German writers who were attracted by the romantic theme of a kidnapped heir and a young man appearing suddenly in a world that was quite new and strange to him.

Kurt Martens wrote a play on the subject of the Nuremberg boy which was produced in 1904, and four years later the novelist Jakob Wassermann wrote a novel around the Kaspar Hauser story. The legend was thus accepted.

But by that time, too, it had been rejected by other students of the Kaspar Hauser story. One of its severest critics was the Scottish writer Andrew Lang, who brushed aside in a gesture worthy of John Knox himself all the so-called romantic aspect of the story. To Lang the youth who appeared in the streets of

Nuremberg nearly eighty years before was a fraud. The word he used was humbug. However, he admitted the possibility that the youth suffered from some form of psychical abnormality. This might have been responsible for a compulsive wanderlust that had been combined with a personality delusion, resulting in a sudden unexplained appearance and a determination to play remorselessly a predetermined rôle.

However, the strong douche of literary cold water poured on the legend by the Scot did not wash it away, possibly because Lang's explosive criticism was ill-timed. It appeared in his *Historical Mysteries,* published in 1904, the same year that the romantic play on the Kaspar Hauser theme was produced in Germany.

As a subject for serious-minded students the Kasper Hauser mystery survived the First World War, and seven years after the close of hostilities a German writer produced a study of the evidence that extended to two large volumes. By that time the legend had been in existence for more than a century.

It is still alive today.

Possibly the real truth of what happened at Karlsruhe one stormy night in the early part of the nineteenth century will never be known for certain, nor will the real origin of the mysterious Kaspar Hauser be decided and determined past all doubt.

The story is unique, and its very quality of uniqueness has helped it to persist. It has attracted attention and created partisans for and against the claims made by those benefactors and sponsors of the young man who, if he was a fraud as Andrew Lang alleged, must have been without parallel as a juvenile actor.

Lang even insisted that the death in the park at Anspach was suicide. If so, it was a singularly curious time to choose, unless a young man who had successfully pulled a good deal of wool over many people's eyes had arrived at a stage where he feared eventual discovery as a charlatan.

However, if this was the case, it seems odd that the same

young man who had persisted for four or five years to win recognition should just as suddenly throw away the final chance of acceptance by the Grand-Duchess Stephanie.

The pros and cons can be argued, as indeed they have been for a century and a half, and one is still left with doubts however much one accepts or rejects the romantic element of the story. Kaspar Hauser is today the name of a person who appeared mysteriously and whose life ended just as mysteriously. The essential mystery is rooted in the fact that nothing has been traced prior to that day in May 1828 when a group of Nuremberg youngsters began to deride and hoot at a strange-looking youth in outlandish dress, apparently unable to form articulate speech.

It is that gap between May 1828 and October 1812, when the Crown Prince allegedly died, that supports the air of mystery; because it remains tantalizingly unoccupied by events that can be verified. Had Kaspar Hauser been the complete fraud Andrew Lang envisaged, then it should not have been impossible to trace his antecedents. The police chief at Nuremberg tried earnestly to find anyone who had known the youth or who was aware of his true identity. He failed.

But he failed in an age when individuals were more susceptible to so-called romantic influences and beliefs than in this far more rational age in the second half of the twentieth century.

Kaspar Hauser remains the mystery he presented to the people of Nuremberg when he first appeared among them : a youth from apparently nowhere that could be located, who died five years later on the threshold of mature manhood, leaving behind a maze of coincidences and enigmas without entirely satisfactory explanations.

However, there is no gainsaying the fascination of such a unique mystery, with its dramatic undertones and suggestions of either brilliant knavery or cruel skulduggery in high places. For such reasons alone the mystery of who was Kaspar Hauser will doubtless continue to challenge fresh minds for a great many years to come.

2

The Mystery of Sir Thomas Overbury

For more than three and a half centuries the murder of Sir Thomas Overbury, in the reign of James the First, has been debated and argued in an atmosphere of mystery and with the avidity with which modern readers pursue the suspense themes and patterns of intrigue in a fictional thriller.

The story of this famous crime has elements of high drama and is shot with colour as well as seams of shade that at times lend the actors involved a look of shabby shiftiness. Like a good many historical mysteries, its roots are concealed in personal desires for advancement and social prominence, and although a great deal of the interests involved are known, it is still possible that much pertaining to the crime and the influences that brought about its perpetration remains unknown even today.

James left his native Scotland and his Scottish throne to be crowned King of England in 1603, after the death of Queen Elizabeth. So a member of the House of Stuart sat upon the English throne, and the country watched with narrowed eyes the close of one era and the opening of another.

James, who was to earn the dubious distinction of being described as the wisest fool in Christendom, was in many ways a solitary man. Stupid in some things, logical and hard-headed in others, he was both temperamental and ingrown as well as far-seeing when his interest was aroused, and capable of temporizing when his personal preferences dictated such a course. A not very happy childhood had left him a grown man who earnestly desired the refuge of friendship.

Unfortunately for himself and for his new kingdom his choice of friends was frequently unwise. That was a failing of most of the Stuarts. Indeed, it was a congenital failing with them that when their heads were soft their hearts were flinty, and when they were hard-headed their hearts melted. They were seldom of sound head and heart at the same time in their lives.

James, as man, was not a person one took to readily. He required a pair of crutches to help his weak spindle shanks, but the only ones he used were provided by the arms of his courtiers. It was embarrassing to stroll with him almost being helped to make each step. Yet James liked strolling.

He also liked talking and at length. Talking was something he did only moderately well, for his salivary glands were defective, and an attentive listener, bending close to catch the words badly pronounced by a great lolling tongue too big for the cage of mouth that held it, was liable to be sprayed with spittly spume.

However, a few of his courtiers showed themselves more ready and willing to suffer the minor indignities that were the price of being a royal favourite than others of greater sensitivity and less avaricious regard for the main chance. One of these was Robert Carr.

Carr hailed from north of the Tweed, like James himself. He had come to Court as a good-looking young page who had been employed by the Earl of Dunbar, and three years after James had adjusted his Scots rump to the English throne he was brought to his feet when, during the course of a tournament put on in the tilt-yard for his royal pleasure, Carr brought himself to kingly notice by a daring display that resulted in his breaking a leg.

James was full of commiseration for the young man with the fair good looks and athletic body. He inquired personally after Carr's progress back to health and later received him into his closest circle of friends. Carr, the son of Sir Thomas Ker, who had little to give his son save his good looks and his fare to London, was a young man who believed in responding when opportunity was knocking. He set himself to snare James's interest and capture his royal goodwill, and he was sufficiently successful that, in the year following the accident at the tourney, he received from James the estates of Sir Walter Raleigh, a man out of favour and languishing in London's Tower, his property confiscated by royal whim, as before long his life was to be.

James's good-looking young yes-man had no compunction about stepping into the shoes of a man who was doomed. In 1607, when he received the confiscated Raleigh estates, Carr was seventeen, though he looked somewhat older. In the next three years, while Raleigh and his family lived as prisoners in the Bloody Tower, Carr was making political hay in James's sunshine. The friendship between the two became very close, and during this period James had few secrets from young Carr. The Scots courtier's influence over James became so marked and effective that in 1610, when Carr was only twenty, he was able to persuade James to dissolve Parliament at a time when the King and his Commons were at loggerheads.

Indirectly Robert Carr, selfish, grasping, swollen with false pride, was to play a part that had a sad influence on the course of English history. He was to aid and abet a Stuart in challenging Parliament. Such seeds were to bear grim fruit in the reign of James's son Charles.

Outside the royal circle of close friends young Carr had other friends. One of these was Thomas Overbury, who was eleven years older and had first met Carr in Edinburgh while on holiday. The pair, Carr and Overbury, presented a striking contrast when in each other's company. Where Carr was fair, Overbury was dark. Where Carr paraded with a bright smile, Overbury wore a tight look on his face that came close to being a frown. Carr purported to be open-natured, while Overbury was secretive and even furtive in manner. Carr appeared to indulge a youthful sense of humour. Overbury was happier nursing grievances, fancied or otherwise, for he was a man capable of deep resentments. When Carr became James's foremost favourite Overbury's friendship was rewarded with employment as the younger man's secretary.

It was a post Overbury filled more than adequately, for he was skilled with his quill, and had served in the royal household as servitor-in-ordinary to James. Born in the same county as Shakespeare, at a place called Compton Scorpion, his literary works have earned him a place among minor English men of letters. His poem *The Wife* had considerable appeal in the first years of the seventeenth century, while his collection of prose writing entitled *Characters, or Witty Descriptions of the Properties of Sundry Persons* established him as a competent essayist. He was also capable of giving vent to more personal feelings that would have been better kept concealed, and he could do this with his pen as well as with his tongue, as he showed when he wrote his *Crumms Fal'n from King James's Table.*

In short, Overbury was the kind of competent secretary who, sooner or later, would prove an embarrassment to a pushing young man bent on climbing the social ladder of his day in double-quick time.

As Carr's secretary, Overbury took care of his friend's correspondence, which often included letters of a secret nature from James as well as State dispatches. It was a curious situation for a man of Overbury's tastes and preferences. He had, when a young man, been friendly with a boy of eleven who had become a page at Court. Now the pageboy had become his master from whom he took orders.

When Robert Carr was eighteen he showed his appreciation of his secretary by asking James to knight Overbury. James was very ready to indulge his favourite in such a small thing. So in 1608 Sir Thomas Overbury rose from his knees, possibly feeling, in his queer way, resentful of this fresh crumb that had fallen from King James's table.

However, before long Overbury had to give value for his knighthood to his master. Hitherto he had penned Carr's letters, including business and general correspondence.

When Robert Carr saw the fresh beauty of a lovely young girl and wished to send her lavish *billets-doux* in the manner of the age, proclaiming his love for her in extravagant terms that were considered the height of good breeding and educated taste, Overbury of the scowling mien was told to get down to a different kind of letter-writing.

So Overbury wrote love letters that held as little meaning for him as a modern greetings card has for the person who composes the doggerel on its inside pages. He found the work extremely distasteful, though he was competent to perform it. The letters he wrote for his master were models of tenderly expressed passion, and they certainly furthered the royal favourite's suit.

But that suit was to a married woman.

Possibly it was because Frances Howard, the daughter of the Earl of Suffolk, was a married woman that Overbury resented her and her influence over young Robert Carr. He might well have feared what her influence on Carr could mean for the secretary. Frances Howard was at the time the Countess of Essex. She had been married to the Earl of Essex when in her early teens, but according to rumours prevailing in Court circles the marriage had not yet been consummated. Perhaps therein lay much of her attraction for the good-looking Robert Carr.

Frances Howard had taken London by storm when only fifteen. She had been presented at Court and had at once become a human showpiece, much like a beauty queen of today. She was five years younger than Carr, who found before very long that he had a rival for the young Countess's favours.

This person was Prince Henry, James's eldest son. Like most men at his father's Court, Henry could not look upon the beautiful face of Frances Howard without believing that she was the most desirable woman he had ever seen.

But Henry had troubles that had nothing to do with an ill-advised love affair which he sought to further. He and his father were too often in disagreement. The father-and-son relationship was a painful one to both, and James was beginning to show contempt for the son who was his rightful heir.

Overbury knew this. He knew all the secrets shared between James and his favourite. He also knew that Prince Henry was a rival to Carr in wishing to obtain Frances Howard's straying affection. For there was no love between the Earl of Essex and his Countess. The marriage had proved a failure in every way. The Earl of Essex was not sorry to go abroad upon State business and find himself freed from the overrated pleasures of life married to a raving beauty of the day.

It was a curious situation, the young wife courted by the King's favourite and the King's son. As for Frances herself, it was the good looks of the fair Robert Carr that appealed to her rather than the more swarthy and certainly less good looks of a young man who one day might be Henry the Ninth of England.

Prince Henry became a young man who was a nuisance to his father. He was also an obstacle in the path of Robert Carr. Overbury was well aware that both his master and the King would be pleased if Henry could be removed from Court – permanently.

Whether Overbury was instrumental in furthering the illness that suddenly laid Prince Henry low can be only conjecture, but in 1612, four years after he had been dubbed a knight, Sir Thomas Overbury was writing letters explaining that the heir to the English throne was sick with a disease generally thought to have been typhoid.

But there is reason to suppose that the disease, whatever it was, had some assistance from poison secretly administered to the ailing Prince. James' son, after whom the father scarcely bothered to inquire, grew worse. Eventually he succumbed despite the skills of physicians sent to attend him.

Prince Henry was mourned by a Court that evinced singularly little surprise at his death. As though not prepared to waste the fresh opportunity presented to him, Carr had more impassioned letters written to his *inamorata* by his secretary. Frances Howard responded encouragingly.

Robert Carr and the Countess of Essex became lovers. Sir Thomas Overbury had done his work well.

The time came when he was to consider resentfully that he had done it too well. For the teenage mistress of Robert Carr decided she wanted to be married to this fair tall man she loved as she had never loved the Earl of Essex. However, there came a forceful interruption to the lovers' idyll. The Earl of Essex returned to England from abroad.

He collected his young wife when he visited London, as he might have collected a favourite saddle horse he had left in a stable awaiting his return, and took her to his home in the country.

Before the young wife left London and the dazzling circle of courtiers, she went secretly to consult a woman known as Mrs. Turner. It is not certain whether Overbury, the efficient secretary in the background attending to his master's interests, procured the introduction. It is at least possible, and certainly not at all unlikely, that the moody secretary had among his London contacts at the time those who could facilitate the young Countess's meeting a woman with the reputation of being a witch who dealt in spells and love philtres and similar unnatural means to further very natural aims. It was an age when the superstitious believed fervently in the efficacy of charms and spells and witches' brews.

Whether Mrs. Turner, despite her dark reputation, was in any sense a witch is extremely unlikely. What is likely is that she had earned a reputation for dispensing certain herbal mixtures, some truly innocent, others more lethal, and she may have had access to known poisons of the day. She was, after all, the widow of a physician. If Prince Henry was, in fact, poisoned, then she could have been the source from which the poison was obtained.

Unquestionably Overbury knew of the woman and her strange and dark practices.

It is equally certain that when the Earl and Countess of Essex left London the latter had concealed either in her luggage or on her person some powders given her by Mrs. Turner. Those powders, when secretly given to her husband, drained him of his normal vitality so that he took little interest in living a normal life.

Frances Howard was left to consider the possible next step in achieving marriage with the King's favourite. It was the grim one of murder.

It has been claimed that, having made the acquaintance of the secretive Mrs. Turner, the Countess of Essex next sought the services of a curious, even more repellent female known by the descriptive name of Cunning Mary.

From Cunning Mary she wanted one thing only. A poison that would kill the Earl of Essex.

Cunning Mary lived up to her name by pretending to go along with the scheme and then, at the last moment, deciding to take no real part in the crime of murder. Furious, the Countess of Essex decided to prosecute the woman who had proved, as she thought of it, untrustworthy. But when word was brought to her that Cunning Mary had intimated that she was prepared to disclose the poison plot the prosecution was dropped.

Cunning Mary had proved cunning enough for her own good.

The Earl and his Countess returned to London and the Court of St. James in the following year, 1613. Seven years had passed since the page had broken his leg in the royal tourney, and Robert Carr was supreme favourite at Court, feared by those on whom he frowned, fawned upon by those who pleased him. He was no longer a commoner. James had created his favourite Lord Rochester in 1610 and was soon to make him the Earl of Somerset. He could match the Earl of Essex in title. Moreover, the forthcoming Earl of Somerset had widespread political influence, for he was Lord Treasurer, and James's favour had resulted in great wealth accruing to the fair and tall young man who still wanted another earl's countess.

More letters passed through the hands of Overbury the secretary, who was busier than ever with the affairs of Lord Rochester. Overbury knew when yet another earl, the Earl of Northampton, who was Frances Howard's grand-uncle, made a secret proposal that his grand-niece should divorce the Earl of Essex upon the grounds of lack of consummation of the marriage. She would then be free to marry the man of her own free choice, Robert Carr.

The proposal was carefully presented to the King. Most probably Overbury had a hand in fashioning the way the proposal took final shape, for he was, up to the very moment that the King was told of the proposed divorce, not only Carr's secretary, but his confidant and friend. James surprised quite a few persons in Court circles by agreeing to the proposal that stemmed from the Earl of Northampton.

It was essential for the Earl of Essex to agree to allow the divorce to be uncontested on grounds acceptable to the Church.

Here James proved himself the friend of his favourite, for perhaps it amused him to take it upon himself to persuade the husband that it was in his interest to help his wife obtain her freedom from him. James may have enjoyed playing the Machiavellian rôle for which his favourite had cast him. Working upon the Earl of Essex's fears as well as his susceptibilities could have given the royal dabbler in marital intrigue a curious pleasure, like an actor who fits perfectly into a part he has been allotted. However that may be, James was sufficiently persuasive, and the Earl of Essex was equally perceptive of the direction in which his own best interest lay.

So the Earl agreed to surrender his Countess without complaint. Indeed, apparently to please James, he agreed to provide any additional grounds for divorce the Archbishop of Canterbury might require.

Which was charitable of him, but hardly noble, and certainly far from manly. But James did not seek to surround himself with manly courtiers. Men of action, who had been at a premium during the reign of Elizabeth, remained out of favour at the Court of the slobbering son of Darnley and Mary Queen of Scots, as the discouraging story of the imprisoned Raleigh testified all too well. Kingship had become a habit with James, rather than a state that imposed obligations to rule wisely on the person wearing the crown. After all, he had been King James the Sixth of Scotland since he was one year old. He couldn't remember when he wasn't a king. So he ruled like the absolute monarch he genuinely believed himself to be, trusting in his divine right to be the possessor of two crowns. Few heads were less fitted to wear either.

However, two persons, vitally concerned with the plot to remove the Countess of Essex from her husband's hearth and home and bring her to live legally under the roof of the man she loved, frowned on the proposed divorce almost as soon as James had approved it.

One was the Archbishop of Canterbury, a very necessary

• •

person to approve such an unusual step. Even James could not flout the opinions of the head of the Church of England. The other was Sir Thomas Overbury.

Overbury had not approved of Rochester's amorous association with the Countess of Essex, but he had hitherto not made the mistake of forgetting that, despite his friendship with his master, he was still the younger man's servant.

But now that he realized Robert Carr intended to make the scheming young Countess of Essex his wife he foresaw danger to himself. Perhaps he sensed that the woman would resent him and the position of trust he held. Perhaps he had certain knowledge that she had become his enemy, and he had knowledge of how Frances Howard was prepared to deal with those she considered stood in her ambitious path.

Whatever the reason, Sir Thomas Overbury expressed to his master and friend, Lord Rochester, his strongly disapproving opinion about the intended divorce and subsequent marriage. For once the blond complexion of the King's favourite was twisted in a scowl. This was an opposition he had not expected. However, he did not quarrel with Overbury. He knew that James had set himself to remove the doubts of the Archbishop in as subtle a manner as the King had used with Essex. He felt that once Overbury realized he was the only one at Court opposed to the divorce and marriage he would give way with good grace.

For once the shrewd Robert Carr was wrong.

James certainly changed the Archbishop's mind. But Overbury remained obdurate, and his opposition to the arrangement became the favourite discussion in Court circles. Indeed, it was said in whispers that Overbury had written a poem he called *The Wife*, and various copies of it in the author's handwriting were circulating throughout London. It was a forceful pronouncement in verse upon the kind of woman an astute young man should take for his spouse, and it extolled the virtues she should possess. Few if any of them could be attributed to Frances Howard, the Court's *femme fatale*.

2—FHM • •

Just why Overbury suddenly became so bitter about the lovely but wanton young Countess still remains a mystery. It was certainly a mystery to James, who was irked by this singular opposition to a man he had knighted only five years before, for James was shrewd enough to know that normally Overbury would not have shown opposition to his King's expressed wish. Overbury was a career courtier. He had, as it appeared on the surface, everything to lose and nothing to gain by remaining pigheaded and obstinate about the divorce and marriage. James, however, was not a man to concern himself with reasons and hidden motives. To him, who had always been a king, there was one simple way to get rid of someone he didn't want to see or hear about – send that person abroad.

James decided it would be best for Overbury, who had spent some time in the Low Countries and France in 1609, to go once more on his travels.

He offered Overbury a diplomatic post of his own choosing, in Paris or in Moscow. The Russian capital at that time was virtually in another world. To have accepted that particular post would have been the equivalent of accepting banishment. Instead of taking the Paris post Overbury thanked the King for his gracious offer and refused both. Which was tantamount to slapping that slobbering royal face, and James knew it. His royal signature was scratched at the bottom of a piece of paper, and on April 22nd, 1613, Overbury was arrested, conducted to the Tower, where Raleigh still languished, and placed in a cell to await trial at the King's pleasure.

That pleasure was likely to be delayed for a considerable time, for James was incensed at having his wishes flouted in the way Overbury had chosen and being made to look something of a fool in the insincere eyes of his courtiers.

It was at this stage that Robert Carr proved false in his friendship to his secretary. He went out of his way to assure Overbury that the King's displeasure would be short-lived. He would see to that. His advice to the man in the Tower was to offer no kind of resistance to James at this stage.

However, it would seem that Lord Rochester, so soon to become the Earl of Somerset, was more keen on keeping Overbury where he was safe from any kind of open action against the divorce and marriage than on removing James's anger against a man who had shown himself unwilling to comply with the royal wishes. For it was shortly afterwards that Sir Gervase Elwys was appointed the new Governor of the Tower of London, and Carr must have known the Earl of Northampton was scheming to bring this about, as he knew that an associate of the ill-reputed Mrs. Turner was made Overbury's personal jailer.

The stage was set for the convenient murder of the Tower's latest prisoner. Just who instigated the murder and who made the individual arrangements is not clear, but certainly it was the lovely Countess of Essex who decided that Overbury should not obtain his freedom and release from the Tower. It took five months to kill Sir Thomas Overbury, and this was achieved by feeding him copper vitriol in regular doses at meal-times, mostly in highly flavoured tarts and concealed in the flesh of well-spiced game. It is believed that the poison was procured from an apothecary named Franklin, who, like Weston the jailer, was known to Mrs. Turner, the same woman who had previously been consulted by the Countess of Essex.

The claim has been made that the conspiracy continued for weeks, small doses of the copper vitriol being given to the prisoner at favourable times, without the knowledge of the Governor. But eventually the poisoning was made known to him. He could have stopped its continuation. He did not. Sir Gervase Elwys turned his head and looked the other way. Obviously because he thought the plot had the highest approval.

He was mistaken.

Although Carr knew what was occurring at meal-times in the Tower it was a secret he did not share with James.

But to keep such a plot secret throughout five months meant bribing numerous servants and workers at the Tower, and undoubtedly the silence of some was obtained by threats of dire reprisals if they spoke of what they knew was happening.

Sir Thomas Overbury died by inches, killed in a most relentless and coldblooded manner. But he had a strong constitution and fought the lethal but sluggish effects of the copper vitriol, though gradually he became weaker and his strength ebbed. If he knew what was happening to him he was given no opportunity of raising the alarm. Everyone attending him was sworn to secrecy. Even a musician named Merston, who carried one of the poisoned game pies to the prisoner, said nothing when, out of curiosity, he poked his fingers under the crust to taste the spicy flavour, and later a fingernail darkened and fell off. The lute player was well rewarded for the loss of a fingernail.

The end of the long-drawn-out death drama came after the dying Overbury's parents had arrived from Compton Scorpion to plead with the King, to no avail. He died after a series of convulsions had racked his wasted body on September 15th, and was interred without delay.

The divorce was speeded up, and Carr, now Earl of Somerset, married Frances Howard in one of the most lavish wedding ceremonies of that lavishly ceremonial reign. Ben Jonson and Thomas Campion both penned Court masques for the nuptial occasion, and Francis Bacon was one of the officials in charge of the lengthy and protracted ceremonies.

That marriage, for which so much had been risked, was the zenith of Robert Carr's astounding career as a royal favourite. It seemed that, once married to his beautiful Frances, his fortunes began to ebb, for he found he could not trust the new secretary appointed by the King. He tried to have the man replaced, and for the first time found himself frowned upon by James. Instead of quickly repairing the breach, the new Earl of Somerset behaved as though he expected the King to change his mind. James did, but not in a way to Robert Carr's liking. He began smiling at a young student from Cambridge whose name was Villiers. On that day Carr's star was firmly in the descendant.

By this time, in 1614, the dead Overbury's poem *The Wife* had been printed. Copies were snapped up as though they were souvenirs and within a twelvemonth from the first printed copies appearing in the shops of the St. Paul's booksellers no less than six editions had been exhausted. The memory of the dead man was being kept alive in a way that was utterly frustrating to those who had schemed his murder.

A year and a half after the Earl and Countess of Somerset had celebrated their memorable nuptials a young man in the Low Countries lay on his deathbed and made a statement which was a confession to providing the sublimate of mercury that had been the final dose of poison administered to the prisoner in the Tower.

The statement found its way from Flushing into the hands of friends of the new royal favourite, George Villiers, soon to be created the Earl of Buckingham, and eventually the Duke of Buckingham, who saw no reason to keep it from coming to James's notice.

Perhaps anxious that no whisper should involve his own royal name with such a scandal, James instructed the Chief Justice, Sir Edward Coke, to hold an investigation. Coke was not half-hearted at conducting a prosecution, as he had shown when prosecuting Raleigh, and in an age when torture was a legal device in the hands of the prosecution he quickly obtained statements which resulted in the trial of Elwys, Mrs. Turner, Franklin, and Weston. All were found guilty of conspiring to murder Sir Thomas Overbury. They were sentenced to death and executed. Thus no scandal touched the King's name.

But plenty was clinging like mud to the names of the Earl and Countess of Somerset.

Indeed, the erstwhile favourite was suddenly in a panic to ensure that he did not become embroiled in the wide scandal. He used his authority to force entry into a house, where papers were found that proved he had known of Mrs. Turner's actions. These papers were destroyed. Unfortunately the servants of the Chief Justice were just as zealous in hunting for proof of the former favourite's complicity. What they uncovered allowed Sir Edward Coke to sign warrants for the arrest of Robert Carr and

Frances Howard. A chain of dire events had come full circle.

Actually, Carr was endeavouring to regain his former status with James at Royston when the officers sent by Sir Edward Coke to arrest him arrived.

"I will not accompany them," he told James.

The King smiled, but it was not the smile Robert Carr had known throughout the past years. It was a smile of amusement, such as the Earl of Essex might have recognized.

"Nay," James said, shaking his head. "If Coke summons me, I must go."

That was telling the tall fair man just how much out of favour he had become. James would do nothing for him. Yet he appeared to act in friendly fashion as Carr prepared to leave, though it is said a group of attendants heard him mutter, as Carr strode from his presence, "I shall never see thy face again."

If he did indeed make such a *sotto voce* remark it was a true enough prophecy.

The trial of the Earl of Somerset and his Countess opened in May of the following year, with Sir Francis Bacon conducting the prosecution. A curious irony this, for he was one of the officials at the prisoners' fantastic nuptial celebrations.

Frances Howard pleaded guilty. She was so involved there was no other course open to her. She was condemned to die.

On the other hand Carr refused to plead. He lost his temper and threatened to make public a great secret if the court proceeded with his trial. Proceedings were adjourned. Word was sent to James, who became upset, possibly because he thought Carr was about to tell the truth about Prince Henry's death. He had word sent hurriedly to Carr. It was tantamount to a deal. If Carr remained silent during the next day's hearing in Westminster Hall, which would be packed with persons of fashion and rank who had paid large sums for seats, no death sentence would be carried out.

The next day Carr remained silent during his swift trial, perhaps not so much because of the verbal promise by James as through fear of the two cloaked strangers who stood behind him, iron-faced men with orders they would carry out. If Carr became indiscreet he would be silenced by a dagger thrust. When the trial ended Carr heard himself sentenced to death.

The royal deal was kept. For six years the Earl and Countess of Somerset lived as prisoners of State in the Tower, where Sir Thomas Overbury had been confined for disrespect to his King, and where he had died in the throes of a wrenching agony because he had opposed a marriage for a reason he had never expressed. At the end of those six dragging years which saw the close of their passionate love idyll, the prisoners were allowed to retire to virtual banishment on their country estate. Frances Howard's beauty faded when she began to suffer from an internal disease from which she eventually died at the age of thirty-nine. It was sometime after his wife's death that Robert Carr once more met the King.

The meeting was at Royston, where James had muttered that he would not see Carr's face again. The years had ensured that, when he stared at his one-time favourite, he saw a face so changed that it was a stranger's.

King James the First of England broke down and cried, not for what time had done to Robert Carr, but for what the past years must mean to a man who had been king for almost too long. To look at Robert Carr, successfully prosecuted by Sir Edward Coke, was to remember that Coke had, a few months later, been removed from his post of Chief Justice for denying the King's right to legislate by proclamation. Raleigh, whose estates had gone to Carr, had been executed in 1618, only a brief time after the Somersets' trial, in the Old Palace Yard at Westminster on an old treason charge. And there was always the memory of Prince Henry.

Robert Carr was a man who walked with the ghosts of the past, and none was closer to him than Sir Thomas Overbury's. There was ample reason for the King's tears, but not for his self-pity.

3

The Mystery of Crown Prince Rudolph

It is possible that the course of European and even world history might have been changed drastically had two pistol shots not been fired one January night in a hunting lodge in the foothills of the Carpathian Mountains.

For one of those shots killed the owner of the hunting lodge, Crown Prince Rudolph of Austria, heir to the Austro-Hungarian throne. When he died the Emperor Franz Joseph was left childless. His heir became the Archduke Franz Ferdinand, whose assassination by a bridge in the small town of Sarajevo was not only to bring the entire continent of Europe to the brink of war, but to push the major nations of the world into the eventual conflict when brinkmanship failed because no one had a notion how to play it.

Had Rudolph lived, the First World War just might have been avoided – at least, for the direct reasons and motives that precipitated it. For Rudolph was unlike other Hapsburgs. He was a free-thinker, a believer in the new liberalism that was finding fashion in the second half of the nineteenth century, and at times he talked and behaved like a revolutionary who was both anti-clerical and basically a republican. How much of this was the fashionable pose of a man who wanted to appear a radical and who enjoyed shocking orthodoxy can only be surmised. For his opinions did not intrude into the two travel books he had enjoyed writing, one in 1881, *Fifteen Days on the Danube,* the record of a fortnight's travelling holiday, and the other three years later, *A Journey in the East.*

Such a son was a great and bitter disappointment to his father.

Rudolph knew this, but he had been for a number of years a son in revolt. At times the revolt came close to open and declared rebellion. He was by nature more interested in the pursuits of literature and natural history than in the study of military techniques and strategies prescribed by his father for the heir to the Austro-Hungarian throne.

Moreover, Rudolph preferred studying languages to reading about the campaigns of successful generals of the past, and he became something of a linguist, so that he was able to converse at first hand with a good many persons who considered themselves enlightened but of whom his father and his father's diplomatic advisers firmly disapproved.

Rudolph the would-be traveller and naturalist and litterateur was twenty-three when he wrote his account of two weeks on the Danube, a river whose name was known throughout the world because Johann Strauss had written a waltz about it fourteen years previously. In the same year that he became an author Crown Prince Rudolph became a husband. On May 10th, 1881, he married Princess Stéphanie, the daughter of the King of the Belgians. The royal newly-weds were at first happy. They were young and filled with the natural enthusiasms of youth. But Rudolph did not mature as the ideal husband, nor as the ideal father after the birth of his only daughter, Elizabeth.

He had his own pursuits, his own desire for philosophic adventures that his father considered dangerous. He and Franz Joseph became gradually more estranged. It was rather like the relationship that had existed between James the First and Prince Henry when James's eldest son was bent on going his own way and making his own friends without regard to his father's wishes. But there was an essential difference. Rudolph was an only son.

Great hopes were centred on him.

He was known to be a young man of considerable talent. It was hoped by his father's advisers that his interests could be directed back into those channels where they would allow him to further affairs of State. Unfortunately the opposite was the case.

Rudolph was a vigorous young man and given to outdoor

pursuits as well as literary pastimes. He found little to please his nature in the strict decorum and protocol of the Court in Vienna, and escaped from it whenever he could, until his absence became the normally accepted thing. His name was mentioned in his father's hearing only when necessary. Crown Prince Rudolph became a subject usually avoided at Court.

This did not mean that Rudolph was without friends or that he lived in any way isolated. He had numerous friends, most of them high-spirited, restive young men and women who shared his views and looked upon the outward trappings of the Hapsburg Empire as so much historic tinsel and gilt that was doomed, in the process of time, to go out of fashion.

Very likely there were good grounds for many of their beliefs, repugnant as they were to Franz Joseph and the advisers who comprised the Emperor's most intimate circle. All the same, Rudolph was neither well-advised nor intelligently perceptive in failing to accept the old-time dictum that rank imposes its own obligations. He was still Crown Prince. To millions throughout the Austro-Hungarian Empire he was a near-godlike figure moulded from a richer clay than the peasants on their strips of land or the burghers in the narrow streets of the picturesque towns. Rudolph failed these people in failing to think of them.

He considered it was being liberated to think only of himself. What he should have perceived was that he was, in the exceptional circumstances of his birth and the age in which he lived, merely being self-indulgent.

The talented Crown Prince, in short, was a free-thinker whose free-thinking was directed in practice only to furthering the sensual preferences and pleasures of Rudolph of Hapsburg. Perhaps this was better understood by his father than himself. However that may be, Rudolph posed a problem to those circles which were intimidated by his unorthodox beliefs and behaviour. In some of these circles he made enemies.

For instance, his anti-clerical views, which he expressed freely and with little thought to the feelings of dignitaries of the Church, were generally believed to have earned him the active enmity of the Jesuits. That very close-knit and disciplined Order was known to have been critical of Rudolph's over-free way of indulging himself and of the friends he made and with whom he disported himself.

Not surprisingly some of the Austrian and Hungarian nobles resented this young man who would one day be their emperor, and it is known that in various directions threats were murmured against him. However, such threats were more the subject of indefinite rumour than of known challenge. Rudolph continued his life for some eight years after his marriage as though what he did, and believed was the business of no one besides himself.

He became estranged from his wife. If this caused him sorrow he quickly recovered, and he was not sufficiently affected by the estrangement as to wish to repair it. He was the idol of a set of young people with money and time to waste, who applauded his liberalism and sponged upon him when they could. It was a youthful set that enjoyed the theatre and hunting and living riotously and even at times recklessly. Their lives served little more useful purpose than to provide employment for foresters and verderers, tailors and gown-makers, and for the grooms and peasants around Mayerling, where the Crown Prince had his hunting lodge.

Indeed, to be invited to spend a brief time at Mayerling was to be accepted as a close friend of Rudolph's. The parties he gave there became notorious and were never referred to within the hearing of the Emperor.

Mayerling was not a great distance from Vienna, which in the eighties of last century was enjoying the prestige redounding to it from the glitter of the Hapsburg Court. It echoed with the melodies of the Strausses, played everywhere from opera-houses to woodland beer-gardens and even in the royal palace of Schönbrunn, with its fifteen hundred rooms and grounds of some seven hundred acres, for although the Emperor could not truthfully be called musical, he would sit stiffly erect through a concert and would nod in waltz time when his favourite tunes were played.

Mayerling was a little world of its own, where Rudolph reigned, where he relaxed, and where upon occasions he was very indiscreet.

Late in January 1889 Rudolph threw his last party at Mayerling.

Upon this occasion the hunting lodge was packed with merrymakers who wined and danced the hours away. The men were the Crown Prince's cronies, numbering those who considered themselves among the *avant-garde* thinkers of their time. Like Rudolph, they enjoyed indulging themselves. The women were the companions one would expect such young blades to have, beautifully gowned creatures of wit and polish who were pleased to find themselves included in the company of the Crown Prince's close friends.

One of the female guests was Marie Vetsera. She had come at the special invitation of the Crown Prince himself. The other female guests threw envious glances at the stately Marie as she crossed the floor of the hunting lodge's main salon. For rumour claimed that the heir to the Hapsburg throne was devoted to her dark good looks and vivid personality.

Rumour also claimed that Franz Joseph and his son had quarrelled bitterly on the subject of Marie Vetsera after the Emperor had told the Crown Prince he must give up his ill-timed friendship with the Viennese beauty.

In Vienna it was generally believed that Rudolph had refused to accede to his father's wishes. Whereupon the Emperor had threatened his son with his gravest displeasure, which could be taken to imply that Franz Joseph was prepared to take steps to make life inside his empire unpleasant for both Rudolph and Marie Vetsera.

It was in a spirit of violent reaction to this quarrel that Rudolph had decided to call his friends to a mid-winter party at Mayerling.

So the friends rode and drove out to the Carpathian foothills and Marie Vetsera left the city to join the Crown Prince. To his friends Rudolph presented an enigma. He was in turn moody and boisterously determined to enjoy himself.

There was hunting in the hours of winter daylight, and at night the hunting lodge was the scene of merrymaking, the guests dining and dancing until the late hours. There were occasions when Rudolph and his friends gathered to sing hunting songs and the latest Viennese popular tunes.

On the surface it was all light-hearted and gay, like a Strauss operetta. But at times the more sensitive members of that winter house-party became aware of a curious tension that impregnated the atmosphere. These were the times when Rudolph appeared moody, sunk in thoughts he did not share.

Unless they were shared with Marie Vetsera.

For the two spent much of the time together away from the others, and what they discussed was never made known. It is possible that, away from Vienna, Rudolph was more keenly aware of how much he had displeased his father, and it is possible that he brooded and became resentful. If so, then it is reasonably sure that Marie Vetsera would have questioned him about his dark moods, and there is no reason to suppose he would have told her less than the truth.

But later there were rumours that Rudolph went to Mayerling expecting trouble of some kind to follow him. It was said he had been threatened. Some said by the angry Jesuits, others that a member of a powerful Austrian family he had personally affronted had sworn to secure satisfaction from him.

Whether he had in fact been threatened or not shortly before he went to Mayerling in 1889 will never be known. Even the few facts on record about that tragic house party were later suppressed except for those that were told by servants at the hunting lodge, and outdoors staff who were on duty on the night of January 29th.

It was on that night that the revels attained their peak. Wine flowed freely, the music was frivolous and inviting to frolic, and the night sped to the gay tunes and shouts of merriment.

The fact that it was noticed the Crown Prince and Marie Vetsera were no longer among the merrymakers did nothing to halt the tempo of the party. On similar occasions Rudolph had assured his guests he wished them to enjoy themselves just as much when he was not with them as when he was actively taking part in the fun and games.

What stopped the party was not the withdrawal of the host, or even his reappearance suddenly among the revellers.

It was the sound of two pistol shots.

Just previously a few of those present had heard, or thought they heard, the sound of male voices in another room of the hunting lodge. The voices were raised in anger, and although the words shouted were not clear enough to be distinguished and remembered there was no doubt about their tone.

In another room a sharp and violent quarrel was taking place. Above the male voices, every now and again, was the shriller voice of a woman, who sounded as angry as the men. Later some of the guests described the female voice as semi-hysterical.

But no one said it was the voice of Marie Vetsera.

Yet whose female voice was it if not hers? And whose male voice was raised in anger other than the Crown Prince's?

That was another of the many questions that have never been answered, and for that reason there is little chance that the mystery of Mayerling will ever be satisfactorily explained now, the best part of a century later.

But if the music and laughter drowned out the sounds of strong and forceful argument coming from another room, the pistol shots were more dramatically demanding. They sounded like thunder claps.

A woman screamed as a violin bow dragged gratingly across catgut, and then there was a sharp and sudden silence that could almost be felt like something physical in the salon where moments before gaiety had reigned.

Within the space of a moment the party was over. The silence continued to drag until the sound of hurrying footsteps on the staircase could be heard. The steps were those of Rudolph's personal valet, a man whose discretion had been well tested in the past and who was devoted to the interests of his royal master.

He had been in the servant's hall when the two shots rang out knell-like in the hunting lodge. With a sharp exclamation of fear he jumped to his feet and ran to the staircase leading past the salon, where the guests were dancing, to the Crown Prince's private apartment.

He approached the door of his master's private dining-room, and hesitated before opening the door. There was no sound from the Crown Prince's apartment. The hunting lodge was quiet, with no music, no sound of animated voices coming from the salon.

The valet was still deciding whether he should or should not invade his master's privacy at such a time, when the door before which he stood hesitating was opened from inside.

Facing the valet was a stranger, and in the stranger's hand was a revolver that pointed at the valet.

"Go away," said the man with the revolver.

The valet still hesitated, aware that some terrible disaster had occurred.

"Away downstairs," the man with the revolver insisted, thrusting the weapon closer to the shocked valet.

The valet turned and hurried away, but not downstairs. As the man with the revolver turned from the open door the valet ran to a wide tapestry that hung at one side of the broad stair landing. He pulled an edge of the tapestry from the wall and concealed himself behind it.

By craning his head he could see into the room beyond the open door where he had been threatened. What he saw almost made him cry out in terror.

Two men were inside the room and they held another man by his ankles and shoulders. The head of the man being carried lolled to one side, and he was plainly unconscious, if not dead.

The man being carried by the two men was the valet's royal master.

Crouched behind the tapestry, he watched the two men carry his master out of his line of vision. But he knew very well they were making for the Crown Prince's bedroom. It seemed a long while that he waited behind the heavy tapestry for the men to return. He continued hiding until he was sure he could reach his master's bedroom unperceived, then he left his place of concealment and stole on tiptoe to the very familiar room.

He entered silently and stood trying to control his breathing without much success. For Crown Prince Rudolph was lying sprawled on the bed's silk counterpane, and there was fresh bright blood on his clothes.

Fearfully he approached the bed and was suddenly relieved to see movement under the bloodstained clothes. The Crown Prince was not dead, only unconscious.

"Your Royal Highness, can you hear me?"

There was no answer to the valet's question. Crown Prince Rudolph was dying. He would not regain consciousness. There is only the valet's word for the strange emptiness of the next tragic hours while Rudolph's life ebbed.

The man claimed to have waited for possibly as much as an hour in the Crown Prince's bedroom. So far as is known he did nothing. Possibly because he heard the sounds of the guests hurriedly leaving, anxious only to be away from the hunting lodge they had been so eager to visit. They left in the freezing January night, scared of being caught up in a scandal and mystery that would rock a great empire.

After that vital hour had passed, according to the Crown Prince's valet, he roused himself to leave his master and return downstairs. He found the door of the large salon open. It was deserted.

Not only had the guests fled. So had the musicians.

The valet went down to the servant's hall. That too was deserted. The footmen and the kitchen staff, made up of peasants from families in nearby villages, had joined in the general exodus from the hunting lodge. The valet had the place to himself.

He knew he could not leave without being sought by the police. He would be questioned about the Crown Prince and the guests. He could do nothing but remain and accept the inevitable. He could not even go for help.

There was no one he could turn to at that hour.

He returned up the stairs to the room where the dying Crown Prince lay, and, as he told the police later, he remained throughout the rest of the night with his master.

By half-past eight there was some light between the trees in the forest beyond the hunting lodge. Crunching his way between them came a man well wrapped up against the biting cold. He stopped suddenly and stared at the blaze of lights coming from the hunting lodge.

"I suddenly knew something was wrong, terribly wrong," he told the police.

He was the gamekeeper Rudolph had told to come early.

Normally he would have gone to the servants' entrance, but this morning he walked in through the open front door. He saw gloves and scarves lying on the floor of the hall and on some of the stairs, as though people had left in a great hurry. He walked to the salon and stood in the doorway, shocked by the disorder he beheld.

Music-stands were overturned, broken chairs lay on their sides, an overturned table remained amidst broken dishes and glassware. Wine bottles had fallen to the floor and their contents had spread from the narrow necks like great stains.

In one corner was a table cover. It seemed to the appalled gamekeeper to be covering something that had been hurriedly concealed.

He advanced and lifted that bunched cover, and found himself staring into the wide eyes of a lovely face. He did not know that he was looking into the face of Marie Vetsera. But he knew she was dead.

She had been shot.

For a few moments the gamekeeper's nerve threatened to forsake him, but he was a man with a normally strong stomach and a sense of responsibility. He dropped the table cover over the dead woman and turned to search the neighbouring rooms and the servants' quarters.

He found no one until he opened the door of the Crown Prince's bedroom.

Crouched in one corner, trembling with terror like a trapped animal, was the valet.

"Do you know what happened?" the gamekeeper asked, lifting the valet to his feet and propping him against a wall.

The valet could not stop his trembling. Through chattering teeth he mumbled, "He's dead—dead," and pointed towards the bed.

The gamekeeper turned and stared at the face of the man who had told him to be on hand at first light to talk over the day's hunt. He left the valet and walked to the bed and saw that he had been told the truth.

He looked round.

"There's a dead woman, too," he said.

The valet nodded as he strove to regain control of himself.

"What happened?" repeated the gamekeeper.

"There were two pistol shots. That's all I know," the valet said insistently.

He repeated those words to the police when they eventually arrived. However, the police had a problem. For the Crown Prince's body had been removed circumspectly to the Hofburg, in Vienna, where some of the finest doctors in the Austrian capital assembled to examine rather fearfully the remains of the Emperor Franz Joseph's heir.

They did not find that the Crown Prince had died quite as simply as had been suggested to them by the chief of police. For instance, if the Crown Prince had died as the result of a shooting tragedy, why was his skull crushed, with slivers of glass protruding from the wound?

It looked as though Rudolph had been hit a savage blow with an instrument resembling a heavy bottle.

When this discovery leaked out it was accompanied by the rumour that the face of the dead man was completely unrecognizable, for the features had been beaten flat against the bones of the head. One possible reason for this rumour gaining currency was the making of a special mask of wax that covered the face when the body of the Crown Prince was prepared for lying in state, as befitted the heir to Franz Joseph.

His valet had vanished. The gamekeeper was not to be located. The body of Marie Vetsera had also been removed to some secret place.

Vienna buzzed with rumours, many of them bizarre and not to be mentioned in the presence of Franz Joseph, who had become a man of stone after learning of his son's violent death. He said nothing about the anguish he felt, he gave no hint as to the bitter savour of his thoughts. Franz Joseph faced a lonely vista of years ahead. He knew that, when he died, there would be no son of his to take his place and become, by the Grace of God, Emperor of Austria, King of Jerusalem, Hungary, Bohemia, Dalmatia, Croatia, Slovenia, Galicia, and Lodomeria. If he was a superstitious man he might have feared for his dynasty. He had every reason to for it was doomed.

Behind the scenes in Vienna diplomats and high-ranking police officials met in conference with a personal adviser of the Emperor.

An announcement was made from the royal palace. It sounded more like a proclamation.

The world was told, in official-sounding terms, that the Crown Prince Rudolph and his friend the Baroness Marie Vetsera had committed suicide in the hunting lodge at Mayerling. Few believed the official statement.

However, interested reporters and others who sought to discover the facts about the strange mystery of the tragedy in the hunting lodge found themselves confronted by a wall of silence. All those friends of Rudolph who had been at Mayerling at the time of the shooting were visited by gentlemen of sober mien and discreet words. They were warned of what would happen if they talked out of turn. In effect, they were sworn to secrecy under a threat of being personally involved in a scandal that could earn them long years in prison.

Not surprisingly no one who had been at Mayerling that fatal January night was found willing to talk about the event. The secrecy of silence, in turn, gave rise to fresh rumours. It was said that members of the Order of Jesuits had gone to Mayerling and killed the Crown Prince and the baroness as a reprisal for Rudolph's attacks on the Roman Catholic Church. This rumour was just as fanciful as the one about the Hungarian nobleman who had felt the Crown Prince had besmirched his family's honour and had gone to Mayerling to settle a most personal debt.

If Rudolph and Marie Vetsera were not murdered by personal enemies, then the only explanation of the two deaths by shooting is suicide.

This of course was the official explanation of the tragedy at Mayerling. What was not explained was why Rudolph felt impelled to destroy himself and also Marie Vetsera. There is reason to support the claim made some time later that the father had given his son an order.

Rudolph was to give up his friendship with the baroness and return to Vienna to live a normal family life and attend to his duties as Crown Prince. In short, Franz Joseph had grown tired of watching his son's display of free-thinking liberalism and wanted it ended.

So he had issued a personal command.

It proved, according to those who sought to probe the motives behind the Mayerling mystery, to be one Rudolph was prepared to resist in the only way that could prove successful against the wishes of his father.

He had given his last riotous house party in the middle of a bitter winter. He had been determined that it was one that would be remembered not only by his father, but by all those who had spoken ill of him to Franz Joseph and, as he conceived it, poisoned the Emperor's mind against him.

But at the last moment Marie Vetsera had not wanted to die.

So there had been a final painful scene, a last bitter quarrel, and the double death by violence brought to a climax a night whose events have never been satisfactorily explained.

Indeed, so adamant was Franz Joseph on concealing the truth as explained in secret to him that he refused to have an official account of findings made *in camera* by the police included in the Vienna State Archives. So today there is no official source by which the truth of the mystery can be discovered.

Was Franz Joseph's reason for refusing to have an official account of the findings rooted in his knowledge that he had brought about his son's death by ordering him to end his liaison with the Baroness Marie Vetsera?

Or was the Emperor's reason for keeping back the truth a very different one? Was he shielding others who had condemned the Crown Prince for follies of which he himself had disapproved most strongly?

It has been claimed that only three or four persons ever knew the full details about the Mayerling tragedy and what brought it about, and these were pledged to secrecy either for family considerations or for what are mysteriously referred to as reasons of State.

But with the passage of time there has evolved yet another rumour, one begun by a royal lady who was close to Franz Joseph and who years afterwards, when the frontiers of the Austro-Hungarian Empire had vanished as certainly as the personages who had made the name Mayerling notorious, wrote and rewrote her memoirs. The part she rewrote most frequently was the story of the Mayerling mystery.

This rumour held that Crown Prince Rudolph had been compelled to commit suicide.

He had the choice of dying by his own hand or by another's and he had decided to take his own life and that of Marie

Vetsera, which had in no way been to the lovely baroness's liking.

Hence the sounds of argument and of a woman's hysterical shouting.

But still unexplained is the mystery of how Rudolph's face came to be so disfigured from a blow with a weapon that could have been a wine bottle. The reason for this must be Franz Joseph's personal order to cover up the facts and avoid anything that could be considered scandalous.

If he did this it was to prevent the scandal reaching his Court circles and giving comfort to his secret enemies who were working to undermine the security of his top-heavy empire.

Whatever the world thought of the Mayerling mystery, and opinion was equally divided between condemnation of the son and of the unrelenting father who belonged to a more strait-laced age, there can be no doubt that it permanently threw a shadow over a lonely man whose throne at times must have seemed very like a subtle instrument of torture.

By nature Franz Joseph did not enjoy personal intrigue and secrets, which curiously may be where he found the strength to be so persistent and determined in keeping unshared the secret of what really happened one January night at the hunting lodge at Mayerling.

4

The Man in the Iron Mask

On a bright summer's day in 1687 a boat put off from the shore of what is now the popular Mediterranean resort of Cannes and headed for Sainte-Marguerite, one of the two Lerin Islands, a short distance from the French coast. In front of the boat stood the provost marshal who was in charge of an armed guard surrounding a prisoner whose face could not be seen, for he kept his head lowered and wore a wide felt hat with a plume.

The boat grounded on the island's beach and the guard sprang ashore. With the provost marshal at their head, they marched towards the main entrance of the rock-girt fortress that a little over forty years before had sheltered Spanish soldiers under the command of Don Miguel Perez. It had finally been stormed by French troops led by the Comte d'Harcourt, who had taken Don Miguel prisoner and replaced the banner of St. James with the lily-decked flag of the Bourbon dynasty.

The guard from the boat came to a halt when their leader raised his right arm. His voice rang clearly in the warm air. "Open in the name of King Louis!"

With a dull, grinding sound the heavy gates of the fortress swung open slowly to reveal, standing to receive the new arrivals, the newly appointed Governor of Sainte-Marguerite, Monsieur de Saint-Mars. He stared fixedly at the uniforms of the guard behind the provost marshal. They were those of the Royal Gendarmerie. Then he looked to the man they surrounded, a familiar figure who kept his head lowered so that the covering over his face could not be seen.

It was a mask concealing the face of a prisoner who had first been brought to Saint-Mars when he had been Governor of Pignerol. Each time he moved the prisoner followed him under heavy guard, like a phantom.

The provost marshal made his formal announcement. "I am delivering into your custody, monsieur, a masked prisoner who will remain masked so long as he is in your charge. This is an order from the King."

The prisoner lifted his head, and Saint-Mars saw the familiar sight of the man who has become known to history as the Man in the Iron Mask. Through the eye slits he could feel the hard gaze. He cleared his throat and spoke to his own waiting guard inside the gates. They moved forward to take the prisoner from the provost marshal's guard.

Some minutes later the great fortress gates clanged shut again, closing on the new prisoner and his regular custodian.

They also closed like a vice on the mystery of the man with the masked face who had been handed into the safe keeping of the governor of that lonely prison in the Mediterranean.

Sainte-Marguerite was one of a pair of small islands off the French coast known as the Iles des Lérins. They were specks in the sea with a romantic past, for hundreds of years before the coming of the Man in the Iron Mask aristocrats of the Roman Empire had built seaside villas on them. In those days the islands had been known as Lero and Lerina, and above the Roman villas rose temples of marble.

By the fourth century A.D. the villas and temples were crumbling and snakes invaded the ruins. For more than a hundred years the islands were twin wildernesses, forgotten and neglected. They had not only gone out of fashion. They had gone from living memory.

Then a man named Honorat, born in Gaul of patrician Roman parents, came to one of the islands. He had been converted to Christianity and felt an overwhelming impulse to live the pious life of an anchorite, away from his fellows. He chose the little snake-infested island in the Mediterranean sunshine as a place where he could devote himself to prayer and contemplation. But the snakes interrupted his devotions.

Honorat prayed for divine assistance in overcoming the snakes, and as a result performed his first miracle on Lerina. He addressed himself to the snakes and within a short while all were dead. The miracle was completed when a tidal wave, completely unknown hitherto in the landlocked Mediterranean, swept over the islands. When the swirling waters receded they bore away the dead snakes. However, with the snakes gone, Honorat found his small island had no drinking water. Again he prayed for help, and this time he was directed to a secret place where a well had been dug. Its water was fresh and clear and cool.

To the other island journeyed Honorat's sister, Marguerite, who had decided that she must live a similar life of devotion. After landing on Lero she felt she must tell her brother what she had done. So she crossed to Lerina, and brother and sister agreed never to visit each other or interrupt their devotions by crossing from one island to the other except when the cherry trees were in bloom.

Honorat and Marguerite were made saints, and according to an ancient legend the cherry trees of the Lerin Islands bloomed every month during their lifetime. Lerina's name was changed to Saint-Honorat and Lero became renamed Sainte-Marguerite, the names by which they are still known.

The Man in the Iron Mask probably saw no cherry trees in bloom during the eleven years he remained in the fortress prison of Sainte-Marguerite. His life became a dull routine, broken only by the occasional visit from Monsieur de Saint-Mars, the governor; he was just as much a prisoner as the mystery man who was in his charge and whose curious mask was never loosened and removed. None of the jailers saw the mystery man's face. The words he spoke to them came muffled so that they could not know the real sound of his voice. When they heard him moaning in moments of despair they crossed themselves and hastened out of earshot.

The years passed with little disturbance. Sainte-Marguerite and its mystery prisoner of State alike seemed forgotten again by the Sun King and his Court. But one day something occurred which filled Monsieur de Saint-Mars with fear. That was the day a fisherman, drawing in his net from the sea under the wall of the fortress, found among the fish and weeds he had dredged up something that gleamed brightly.

It was a silver plate with little marks scratched across its bright surface, as though with a knife point, little marks that the fisherman realized was writing. Someone had scratched a message across the plate and flung it into the sea in the one place where it might be found.

However, the fisherman could not read.

He took the plate with its message to Monsieur de Saint-Mars and explained how he had come to find it. The Governor of Sainte-Marguerite looked at the scratch marks on the plate for a long time before asking his first question.

"Have you read the message on this plate?"

The fisherman shook his head. "I cannot read, your honour," he confessed.

Saint-Mars looked at him sternly.

"Have you shown this plate to anyone else?" he asked.

"I brought it directly to you, your honour," the fisherman replied, "as soon as I had landed my catch."

"Why to me?"

"I saw that on it."

The fisherman pointed to a fleur-de-lys crest on the plate. That crest was the royal insignia of the Bourbons.

It is said Saint-Mars gave the fisherman a piece of gold and told him, "Take this and forget what you have found. Just remember that you are a terribly lucky man."

Looking from the golden louis in his hand to the still stern governor of the prison, the fisherman asked falteringly, "You mean I am a lucky man to be paid in gold, your honour?"

"No," said Saint-Mars. "You are lucky because you cannot read."

Was the message of the silver plate a desperate plea thrown into the space outside his dungeon wall slit by the Man in the Iron Mask? Even the plate with the royal crest and its unknown message have passed into legend that only makes the curious mystery more baffling.

Saint-Mars was a man who could keep a secret, especially a royal one. His long vigil over his unknown prisoner was in due course rewarded when he was promoted from Governor of the lonely island of Sainte-Marguerite to Governor of the most dread and formidable fortress prison in France, the notorious Bastille, in Paris.

However, there was a condition attaching to this promotion. When Saint-Mars left the sunshine of the Mediterranean for the gloomy precincts of the Bastille he did not travel alone. He was accompanied by his very special prisoner, the Man in the Iron Mask.

On this point there was no room for doubt, for seventy-one years later, exactly twenty years before a mob stormed the Bastille and so made the first violent move in what was to grow into the French Revolution, a diary was published in Paris. It was a slim volume of personal reminiscences by a certain Etienne de Jonca, who had been appointed a lieutenant at the Bastille at the time of the arrival of Iron Mask. He had died three years after the mysterious prisoner.

In the diary appeared the following entry for September 18th, 1698:

"At three o'clock in the afternoon Monsieur de Saint-Mars, Governor of the Bastille, arrived from the island of Sainte-Marguerite. He brought with him in a litter one of his former prisoners at Pignerol whose name is not mentioned and who is constantly masked. On his arrival he was put in the Tour de la Basinière till dark. At nine in the evening I conducted him myself to the third room in the Tour de la Bertaudière, which I had taken care to furnish properly before his arrival, according to an order received by me from Monsieur de Saint-Mars. In conducting him, I was accompanied by Monsieur de Rosarges, who came with Monsieur de Saint-Mars, and took care of and attended the prisoner whose table was furnished by the governor."

Unfortunately Etienne de Jonca did not feel, at that time, impelled to enlarge upon the subject of the mysterious prisoner. He remained a lieutenant of the Bastille for the next five years, at the end of which time he made another entry in his personal journal. In this entry he referred to the prisoner's mask, but did not give him a name.

The entry read :

"Monday, November 19th, 1703. The unknown prisoner, whom Monsieur de Saint-Mars brought with him from the island of Sainte-Marguerite, where he had been a long time under his care, and who has always been masked with a mask of black velvet, found himself worse yesterday, in coming from Mass, and died this evening at ten o'clock without any great illness. Monsieur Girault, our chaplain, confessed him yesterday; his death being sudden, he had not an opportunity of taking the Sacraments, but our chaplain exhorted him a few minutes before he expired. He was buried on Tuesday, November 20th, in the burying place of our parish of St. Paul. His burial cost forty livres."

An almost laconic reference to the passing of an unknown whose identity remains one of the great mysteries of history. But in making it de Jonca added his own piece of mystery. He had referred to a velvet mask that was always worn by the prisoner, not a mask of metal. Historians and more romantically minded writers have argued about the material of which this mask was made for more than two hundred and fifty years. Some have accepted de Jonca's description, others, like Alexandre Dumas, supported the claim that the mask was indeed of iron. It is more than likely that the mask was a sadistic contrivance with a metal collar and metal stays to which a concealing pad of shaped velvet was fastened, to make it possible for the person wearing it to eat and breathe. But a material such as velvet would have worn out with day-to-day use, and there is no record of the mask being renewed or having to be. Apart from de Jonca's private note made at the time of the unknown's death there is no factual proof, only legend that is as enduring as iron itself.

However, the parish register of St. Paul contains an entry that actually gives the mystery prisoner a name. Unfortunately the name in this entry merely serves to confuse rather than clarify the prisoner's identity.

This register entry reads :

"In the year 1703, on the 19th day of November, Marchiali, aged forty-five years or thereabouts, died at the Bastille. His body was interred in the burying place of this parish of St. Paul on the 20th of the said month, in the presence of Monsieur de Rosarges, Major of the Bastille, and Monsieur Reilh, the surgeon, who accordingly sign this."

Neither of the Bastille officials who signed the register had the name Marchiali altered, but so far as can be traced no one of that name could have been the prisoner known to history as the Man in the Iron Mask.

On the other hand, it is known that Saint-Mars did have in his keeping for long periods two prisoners whose names were Douger and Mattioli. Saint-Mars was the governor of three fortress prisons before being appointed Governor of the Bastille. He spent the years from 1664 to 1681 in charge of the jail at Pignerol, then for six years he was the Governor of Exiles, moving on in 1687 to Sainte-Marguerite. He remained Governor of the Bastille until his death, when a great many secrets passed away with him.

One of these was the real identity of the Man in the Iron Mask.

What is known is that Saint-Mars invariably treated the masked mystery prisoner with the greatest respect, as though he were of royal blood or were a State prisoner of high rank.

Why the prisoner at Pignerol named Douger, who was arrested in 1669, was thrown into jail and apparently forgotten is not known. But he was without doubt in Saint-Mars' custody at Pignerol. So was Mattioli, arrested ten years later, in 1679. The likelihood is that one of these men was the notorious Iron Mask, who followed Saint-Mars each time he changed governorship. Allowing for a possible misspelling of the name Mattioli in the St. Paul's parish register, it would seem that de Jonca had heard of Mattioli arriving at Pignerol while Saint-Mars was governor and had heard, furthermore, that no reference was to be made to the prisoner's identity. So no such reference was made in his journal, even after five years. But a name had to be given to the clerk who filled in the parish register and procured the signatures of the surgeon and the officer described as the major. De Jonca could have been the officer who supplied the few details necessary for the entry in the parish register.

However, even this is not conclusive. It would seem to put too much emphasis on a mere clerical error.

Saint-Mars himself aided, rather than otherwise, the growing confusion about his masked prisoner's identity. Indeed, he frequently wrote about him, but invariably referred to him as the Mask or the Man in the Mask, and on one occasion he confessed that he had deliberately circulated stories about the prisoner that were fabrications. His description of these was "fairy tales", in the circumstances not the most apt of terms.

But Saint-Mars could have had a reason for behaving in this deliberately misleading manner. It is possible that he did not know his prisoner's identity, but endeavoured to demonstrate to whoever was responsible for the man being put in his custody that he was actively working to maintain the prisoner's anonymity.

That the prisoner was a high-ranking prisoner of State, whose identity had to be kept a secret for State purposes, was of course known to the man who became his chief guardian from the time he arrived at Pignerol, in Piedmont. For the prisoner to escape, or for his identity to become known, would have meant death for Saint-Mars. So far as it known, he treated his prisoner with an aloof deference and did his best to make the unknown's lengthy incarceration less onerous and degrading than it would otherwise have been. After all, the prisoner might be released one day. That could be a sad day for Saint-Mars if the released man, free of his mask, remembered only suffering and hardship.

Undoubtedly the legend about the masked prisoner began

with Saint-Mars himself, who did not describe the actual mask. It was Voltaire who was responsible for perpetuating the legend that the prisoner was, in fact, a natural brother of Louis XIV, who was imprisoned by the King so that he could not become a rival for the throne of France. Voltaire also claimed the prisoner's peculiar mask, which was a kind of total headgear, was actually made of iron.

From that day the mystery prisoner was, to the French, *Masque de Fer* – Iron Mask. To the rest of the world he became the Man in the Iron Mask.

Dumas took over the Voltaire claim and wrote a novel around the conception of a twin brother of Louis XIV who was imprisoned when he grew up and kept with his face perpetually concealed by an ingenious mask made of iron.

Such a mystery prisoner was explained away by other writers who were challenged by the peculiar circumstances. The mother of Louis XIV, Anne of Austria, was said to have had a son by the English Duke of Buckingham at the time of his visit to France in 1625. The baby was, according to this claim, taken from the royal apartments by Cardinal Mazarin, who made himself responsible for the child's upbringing and education. Mazarin died in 1661, and afterwards the King had the Cardinal's charge, who was thirteen years older than Louis, imprisoned after a mask-like piece of special headgear had been riveted to the prisoner's neck.

For the believers in this theory there is the period of years between 1661 and 1679 to be explained, if that was the year when the Man in the Iron Mask first was handed over to the custody of Saint-Mars. In any case, as other writers have pointed out, this theory would have had the prisoner over eighty years of age at the time of his death in the Bastille. This is extremely unlikely and runs counter to the evidence of de Jonca.

Others have claimed that, while this story is true in the main, and that Cardinal Mazarin did in fact take care of a child born to Anne of Austria, it was Mazarin himself who was the boy's father. This claim is even less likely except in one particular.

The claimants argue that this child was born in 1644, a much more likely date than twenty years earlier.

More fanciful theorists purport to have found reason to believe that the Man in the Iron Mask himself became a father, and that his son was smuggled away to the island of Corsica where he became known as de Buona Parte, married in due course, and so founded a family that later produced another child who was destined to become famous – Napoleon Bonaparte.

But such a theory is little more than an extravagant flight of fancy, and certainly the republican artillery officer who later became Emperor of the French had no illusions about being descended from royal blood.

He looked upon the House of Bourbon as his arch-enemy.

The masked prisoner has also been identified as at least two other French noblemen. One was the Duc de Beaufort, the second son of another duke, the Duc de Vendôme, who was descended from the royal house as an illegitimate son of that warlike Henry of Navarre who decided Paris was worth a Mass and became Henry IV.

But this claim falls down on close examination, for the Duc de Beaufort was born in 1611, and was killed nearly sixty years later by the Turks, in June 1669, at the siege of Candia. This was said to have been witnessed by the Marquis de Saint-André Montbrun. However, the slaughtered duke's body was never recovered, and it is probably for this reason that the rumours began which linked him to the unknown masked prisoner. But an examination of the relative dates shows that this possibility is even less likely than the claim that the masked prisoner was sired by the Duke of Buckingham.

Another royal personality fitted to the legend, although imperfectly, is the Comte de Vermandois, who was the son of Louis XIV and the Duchesse de la Vallière. But he was born as late as 1667.

He died in 1683, when only sixteen, according to the records, but although Louis loved this son it is known that on more than one occasion he made his father terribly angry by actions which were never explained to the Court.

Even more unlikely is the claim put forward by other theorists who had found reason, as they considered, for believing that the Man in the Iron Mask was none other than the great dramatist, Jean Molière, who, from being a strolling player, became the most penetrating satirist of his age. He is alleged to have gravely upset the King, who decided to teach the man of savage and unbridled wit a lesson he could take the rest of his life to learn.

But there is no foundation for this high-flown piece of fancy, and in any case Molière was born in 1622 and was over fifty when he died in 1673. Such a prisoner would not have lived at Pignerol or on Sainte-Marguerite without writing and what he wrote would not have been lost to the world unless it was deliberately destroyed. There is no record of Saint-Mars having works by his prisoner burned.

The theorists did not limit their fanciful flights to French or half-French subjects. At one time there was a strong claim put forward that the masked prisoner whose identity was never revealed by Saint-Mars was the English Duke of Monmouth, whose army of Protestant yokels was defeated at the battle of Sedgemoor, in Somerset, in 1685. Monmouth was a natural son of Charles II and he was sentenced to be executed for leading the rebellion against his uncle, James II. A legend grew up about a substitution of another prisoner for Monmouth on the day he was to be executed in London on Tower Hill. According to rumours circulating soon after Monmouth bowed under the headsman's axe before a great crowd, his uncle the King had made a secret pact with the King of France to conceal his ill-advised nephew. Once Monmouth was in France, King Louis decided his face must never be seen by any who could recognize him. So he became the Man in the Iron Mask.

The entire legend was given considerable support by two persons, a Frenchman and an Englishwoman. The former, Saint-Foix, purported to have learned that, shortly before his death, Charles II had made his brother James swear that, despite any folly into which Monmouth might be led by unwise counsels, he should never be called to answer for his actions with his life. According to Saint-Foix, James had promised his dying brother that nothing Monmouth did would make his life forfeit.

The Englishwoman's part in furthering this legend of Monmouth being the Man in the Iron Mask was much more direct. She claimed to have had Monmouth's grave opened secretly, and to have been shocked by seeing a stranger's face on the severed head. She was Lady Wentworth, whose word carried considerable weight, but if she did peek into Monmouth's coffin she very likely saw the result of shock and muscular distortion on familiar features wasted by death, which made them appear a stranger's and for her, in her undoubted highly emotional state at the time of such a clandestine exhumation, unrecognizable as those of the unfortunate James, Duke of Monmouth. If Monmouth had only waited three years he might have paraded his yokels to London without having to strike a blow. But if he was, in truth, the Man in the Iron Mask he must have suffered agonies when, in 1688, the Protestants William of Orange and his Stuart wife Mary landed at Lyme Regis to be acclaimed as dual monarchs while James II took the first ship available to sail for France and exile.

But such are the ironies of history.

However, the widespread belief that Iron Mask was a man with some kind of English background persisted when other claimants advanced the theory that the famous prisoner was Eustache Douger, who was sent to Pignerol, where he is known to have acted for a time as valet to another prisoner. This was Nicholas Fouquet, who had received a life sentence for robbing the State of a vast fortune while in charge of national finances under Cardinal Mazarin.

Douger – or Dauger, as the name is sometimes spelled – was no more than a *nom-de-guerre,* according to those who believe he was Iron Mask. They have given him the identity of an

Abbé Pregnani, who was known to have been in England at one time endeavouring to convert Charles II to Roman Catholicism. He was unsuccessful, and returned to the Continent via Dunkirk, where he was supposedly seized and sent secretly to Pignerol. Some of the supporters of this theory have even advanced the suggestion that the Abbé Pregnani was able to obtain such close audience with the English King because he was actually Charles's son.

At best it seems merely a variant of the Monmouth theory.

Much more likely is the now generally held belief that the mysterious prisoner was an Italian count named Mattioli, who became one of the Duke of Mantua's principal ministers and was the chief architect of a plan to lease a frontier fortress to the French at a price. The fortress was the strategical one of Casale, and the price was a hundred thousand crowns.

The French king was not averse to making the deal. However, he not only lost interest in it, but became angry with Mattioli when he learned that, on behalf of the Duke of Mantua, the count was setting up a league of Italian States to challenge the supremacy of France.

Secret agents were sent by Louis to kidnap the double-dealing Italian. He was to be brought back to France alive.

The men despatched from France crossed into Italy and eventually came up with Count Mattioli in Turin, where he was making an attempt to persuade the Duke of Savoy to join the proposed Italian league.

He was seized and spirited out of the city and back across the French frontier. To ensure that the truth of this secret mission never became known, Louis ordered the new prisoner of State to be masked and imprisoned at Pignerol. However, the secret of the kidnapping was breached when, a few years later, an account of the Casale conspiracy was related in a volume published in Cologne. In this the story of the kidnapping of the man who broke faith with Louis was told for the first time.

If the Duke of Mantua made any protest to King Louis about the treatment of Mattioli no record exists today, for twenty-eight years after the incident Mantua was captured by the Austrian troops of Prince Eugene, who was an ally of Marlborough's in the War of the Spanish Succession, and in that same year, 1707, he had most of the Mantua State archives sent to Vienna. Later they vanished.

From that time a conspiracy of silence seemed to involve anyone who might know the truth. Saint-Mars, according to an elderly official at the time of the French Revolution, had intimated to his father that the masked prisoner had been at one time a minister at the Court of Turin. But there was no further support for the claim that Saint-Mars had broken the habit of a lifetime.

Louis XV was equally silent on the subject except, according to rumour, when he spoke of the famous prisoner to the Duc de Choiseul, a favourite of his. Even then, the rumour claimed, he merely intimated that the unknown was a minister from an Italian state. But this may have been no more than fitting a piece of an incomplete jigsaw puzzle into a missing space.

All the same, the weight of evidence points to the Man in the Iron Mask being the kidnapped count, and to the mask being of velvet, at least in the later years of his life. Support for this was provided by a fellow-officer who served at the Bastille with de Jonca. His name was Chevalier, and after the masked prisoner had been buried he related how his room in the fortress prison was virtually destroyed to remove all trace of his lonely tenure. Its walls were thoroughly scraped, the ceiling pulled down, and the floor-boards removed and burned with the furniture. All metal fixings and tableware were removed and melted down. In this way any trace of his having existed was destroyed. His clothes and mask were burned.

Yet it is a fact, as another prisoner from Sainte-Marguerite confirmed, that the masked man ate his meals from a silver plate, was treated with some deference by Saint-Mars, the governor, who also provided the unknown with costly clothes. Moreover, the man in the mask spoke several languages in a cultured voice and was grey-haired.

Beyond a few details such as these lies only conjecture. There was a chance of learning the truth at the time of the taking of the Bastille, on July 14th, 1789, but secret records were destroyed or vanished and nothing remained in the masked prisoner's room in the Tour de la Bertaudière to point to his ever having spent five years and two months there, concealed from the world that had known him.

5

Mystery of the "Mary Celeste"

In the year 1861, that saw the opening of the American Civil War, a brigantine was built stoutly and with plenty of "blue-nose" know-how on the stocks of a shipbuilding yard in Parrsborough, on the coast of Nova Scotia. Just before she was ready for launching a sign-writer was told to climb over her bows and paint her name. It was a rather intimidating name: *Amazon*.

Not that the new ship looked very warlike, even in a feminine way. She had two masts and her length was just two feet under an even hundred. Her beam was a quarter of her length, twenty-five feet. She was of modest tonnage. It was registered as 282 tons.

When at last she glided down the slipway and rode for the first time with her keel under water she did not look like a vessel whose future would be clouded in mystery. But today she is remembered as a vessel whose name became synonymous with one of the most puzzling mysteries of the sea.

But that name is not *Amazon*.

It is an age-long superstition among deep-sea sailormen that to change a ship's name is to invite bad luck to attend her subsequent career.

After the *Amazon* had been in service for some years as a sailing vessel carrying general cargo up and down the Atlantic seaboard and occasionally to Europe she was sold and her new owners had her name changed. The old name was painted out, and instructions were given for the name *Mary Sellers* to be substituted.

Possibly the new sign-writer was a French-Canadian. In any case, he must have misunderstood his instructions, for the name he painted on the brigantine was *Mary Celeste*. A curious name, half English, half French. Indeed, for many years after the mystery attending one of her voyages across the Atlantic, she was known as the *Marie Celeste,* an all-French name. But this name was incorrect, although she is often referred to in modern times by that mistaken name.

For eleven years she ploughed the Atlantic sea lanes familiar to her until she brought up, in November 1872, in New York, where she was manoeuvred alongside a quay, and when the gangplank was lowered her master, Captain Benjamin S. Briggs, went ashore to see the agents and learn what cargo she was to take aboard and where she was to sail it.

Captain Briggs was not only the brigantine's master; he was part owner. His home was aboard the *Mary Celeste.* When her anchor was winched aboard and her sails were unfurled Mrs. Briggs and her young daughter, who was two years old when the *Mary Celeste* tied up in New York on that November day, were installed in the captain's quarters.

The agent greeted Captain Briggs with a friendly nod and told him of the cargo waiting to be moved to the *Mary Celeste*'s hold.

"It's commercial alcohol this time, Captain. You're to deliver it in Genoa."

Whatever he felt at this news, Captain Briggs could not have been overjoyed. There were less tricky cargoes to be carried than alcohol, whatever its quality, and there were more pleasing routes to be followed than crossing the Atlantic with winter coming on in a slow sailing vessel whose deck could be covered from stem to stern in thirty good paces.

"How soon do you want me to sail?" he asked the agent.

"As soon as her hatches are battened down. We'll start loading without delay."

That evening the *Mary Celeste*'s master told his wife, "I'm going to see Moorhouse. I saw the *Dei Gratia* was in port. David will expect me to look in on him."

He went ashore, found his friend Captain David Moorhouse of the brigantine *Dei Gratia,* and the two sailing masters had dinner together. Neither knew it was the last time they would

see and talk to each other. Yet, by one of those ironical coincidences that are frequently encountered in real life, and make it
even more absorbing than the most carefully plotted fiction, it
was to be Captain Moorhouse who first gave to the world the
story of the mystery surrounding his friend's ship and her crew.

The next day seventeen hundred barrels of commercial
alcohol were taken aboard the *Mary Celeste* and stowed in her
hold. The weather turned bad. Captain Briggs, who had spent
his life at sea, was thirty-seven years old, and had used his
savings to buy a share in his command, decided it would be too
risky to head for the open ocean. He dropped anchor off Staten
Island, in the mouth of New York harbour, and waited until
the weather changed.

He had to wait two days. That was anything but a promising
beginning for the voyage.

However, on November 7th the weather changed. The wind
dropped and the sea grew calmer. Captain Briggs gave the
order for the brigantine's anchor to be raised and stowed. A
short while later the *Mary Celeste* was dipping her bows and
heading in an easterly direction on a southerly tack, bound for
the Mediterranean and the Italian port of Genoa, the birthplace
of Columbus.

As the *Mary Celeste*'s topsails vanished over the horizon she
was sailing into a mystery that still challenges many to solve it.

One of the first to accept the challenge was David Moorhouse. When he left New York he was carrying a cargo to be
landed at Gibraltar. Like Captain Briggs, he had to take note of
the prevailing weather conditions, and he too started on a
southerly tack.

Crossing the Atlantic in those days by sail could take up to a
month. Already the early steamships were cutting down the
time, but the sailing-ships carrying general cargo were cheap
and, despite the longer time taken on voyage, they could still
compete with the new steamers as carriers of merchandise.

It was almost a month after the *Mary Celeste* had up-
anchored off Staten island that the lookout on Captain Moor-

house's *Dei Gratia* reported a sail. The time was around three in the afternoon of December 5th, 1872. Before very long the light would be failing. There was a smudge of smoke against the sky far to starboard, where a German steamer continued her course to the West Indies.

Her captain had signalled to the sailing vessel just reported by the *Dei Gratia's* lookout, but had received no answering signal. He had decided to continue on course.

Captain Moorhouse signalled, and he too received no reply. He gave orders to his second mate, named Wright, to move closer to the other sailing vessel, while he studied her through his telescope.

As the *Dei Gratia* altered course her captain noted the deserted deck of the vessel he was overhauling. There was no one at her wheel, and she was yawing badly. There was no distress signal flying from her masthead, but Captain Moorhouse had a feeling that something was very wrong with the ship seen through his telescope. Her flapping canvas and deserted appearance hundreds of miles from the nearest land, in a position south-east of the Azores, betokened trouble.

He kept the telescope trained on her until he could make out her name.

Mary Celeste.

Captain Moorhouse closed his telescope with a snap.

"Mr. Deveau!" he called.

The first mate came hurrying.

"You will take a boat and boarding party," Captain Moorhouse told him, "and find out why that brigantine appears deserted."

"Aye-aye, sir," said the *Dei Gratia's* first mate, and turned away, calling to some of the crew.

The light was growing poorer as the *Dei Gratia's* boat covered the distance between the two brigantines alone in mid-Atlantic. Captain Moorhouse watched his men clambering aboard the other ship, and waited impatiently for Deveau to return and report what he had found.

It was a puzzled and unhappy first mate who returned to seek out his captain and tell him of the mystery of a ship deserted by her crew with no apparent reason for their leaving. Deveau had found no one aboard the *Mary Celeste*. Her single boat, big enough to carry her crew of seven as well as the captain and his wife and baby daughter, was no longer held on its davits.

In the short time he had been aboard Deveau had run a critical seaman's eye over the state of the deserted ship. He had found almost nothing wrong with her. There was some damage to the bows, but it hadn't looked serious. There was also a good three feet of seawater swilling about the barrels in the hold, but that was not a danger level, and so far as Deveau had been able to tell she was not dangerously shipping water.

Moreover, there were plenty of supplies aboard. The quick glance he had taken had shown supplies for about six months. He had looked into the captain's quarters. There he had seen a pipe on a ledge and some pieces of feminine jewellery on a shelf, items one would have expected the captain and his wife to pick up if they were in a hurry to make a sudden departure from the brigantine.

Deveau had even noticed some of the Briggs baby's toys lying on a cabin floor, where presumably they had been left when the child ceased playing with them. He had opened a cupboard door to be confronted by garments belonging to the captain and Mrs. Briggs hanging normally from their pegs.

Indeed, everything aboard the *Mary Celeste* seemed normal. This was the basic mystery surrounding the ship and what had occurred to send her occupants away in the only boat – if that was how they had left her.

When Captain Moorhouse heard of what his first mate had found aboard his friend's ship he decided to take the *Mary Celeste* into port.

"We'll put a party aboard her, Mr. Deveau," he declared, "and we'll take her to Gib. You'll go back and steer her."

"We'll lose time," the first mate pointed out.

"That can't be helped. She's deserted, we'll salvage her, and they can start arguing about her when we tie up and the Gib harbour master comes aboard."

Captain Moorhouse paused, giving his first mate a hard glance, and asked, "What do you think happened, Mister?"

Deveau shook his head.

"I can't be sure of course," he said. "But I noticed that their sounding rod was lying near the pumps, Captain."

"You think they were worried about the water in the hold? That it?"

"I think they were led to believe the water was rising, and as there was a woman and her child aboard the captain gave the order to take to the boat."

"You'll have to appear before a salvage court, Mister," Captain Moorhouse reminded the first mate. "Is this what you'll tell them?"

Deveau nodded. "Aye, sir. This is what I believe must have happened."

"How long ago?"

"That I can't say till I've made another examination," said the first mate.

He had plenty of time to make up his mind on the long haul to Gibraltar. But it was a puzzling task, as he discovered when he examined the neatly kept log book, found in its regular place, but only made up to some ten days before she was taken in tow by the *Dei Gratia*. The entries were typical seamen's notes, containing a minimum of information, and there were not more than seven of them made from the time the *Mary Celeste* had pulled eastwards from Staten Island.

One entry said briefly, "Got in Royals and top G. sail," leaving any mariner reading it to understand why. Another, presumably referring to the *Mary Celeste*'s course, if not to the prevailing wind, was "E.S.E."

The one word "Rainy" was a third entry. "9 knots" was one referring to the vessel's speed.

The last position recorded was "36 N 56, 27 W 20". The day

was November 24th, the last day the log book was brought up to date, in any sense of the term. There was, however, a chalked record on the nearby slate. This was for the next day. The chalk entries on the slate were normally transferred at a convenient time later to the log book. That had been the usual custom in such sailing-ships for a great many years.

The chalk entry on the *Mary Celeste*'s slate gave the additional information to the puzzled Deveau that at eight o'clock in the morning of the following day after the last log book entry had been made the brigantine was six miles north-north-east beyond the eastern tip of one of the Azores islands. This was the small island of Santa Maria.

It naturally occurred to him to consider the possibility that the captain and crew of the *Mary Celeste* had abandoned ship shortly after that chalked information was made on the slate. But ten days earlier the level of the water in the hold would presumably have been lower than it was when the sounding rod was dropped beside the pumps. There was no valid reason that the first mate of the *Dei Gratia* could see for assuming that the *Mary Celeste* had been deserted as long as ten days before she was found.

There was also the detail of her sails at the time Captain Moorhead stood viewing her coming closer in his telescope. She was on a port tack at the time, yawing wildly, but her foretopmast-staysail and jib were set to starboard. She would hardly have reached the position where she was found under such a rig, for Captain Moorhead had logged his own ship's position at the time of coming up with the *Mary Celeste*.

This was 38 N 20, 17 W 15. In short, she was five hundred miles from Santa Maria in the Azores. Only the capable handling of her crew could have brought her across that distance. However, to writers not so sea-minded as Deveau and his captain, there has apparently been a curious landlubber's logic in asserting that the missing boat was lowered, and the ship's company left in it, shortly after that last chalk mark was made on the logging slate.

On the journey to Gibraltar a further survey was taken of the state of the *Mary Celeste,* and some new items of interest were discovered.

Apparently Benjamin Briggs had left in the ship's boat with his crew and family, taking with him some of the *Mary Celeste's* stores, but not enough for a journey of lengthy duration. However, he had been careful to collect, before stepping into the launched boat, his sextant, which would be a necessary aid to navigating, especially in winter, and also the *Mary Celeste's* ship's papers, a matter that would be of deep concern to the master of any ship.

But he had not pocketed his watch before leaving, and he had not bothered to pick up some loose money found in his cabin. In the crew's quarters there was the same apparent readiness to forgo personal items when leaving the *Mary Celeste,* and perhaps it was more marked in their case, for sailormen received little in cash pay a hundred years ago.

The *Mary Celeste's* crew had left their sea-chests, a costly item in any sailor's inventory of personal effects, and there was no sign of the chests being rifled or hurriedly emptied. In each case the chest remained with its contents neatly arranged. Sailormen usually took the trouble to pocket their favourite pipe. But several pipes were found in the *Mary Celeste's* fo'c'sle, as well as rolls of tobacco.

There had, in fact, been no attempt to remove the kind of personal possessions one would have expected the members of the crew to push into their pockets before leaving the ship.

But one factor that did invite consideration was the hatch cover that had been removed and was found lying on its other side. Added to the additional factor of a barrel below that open hatch being found damaged, it was to invite a number of widely varying theories about what had happened, ranging from alcohol fumes blowing off the hatch cover and creating panic, to the crew having forced open the hold and reached the alcohol, their first stage towards outright mutiny.

This last picture of events was at first supported by the cutlass that was found lying on the deck. The weapon's blade had some dark red stains on the weathered steel. Unfortunately for the theorists with lively imaginations these stains were later, in Gibraltar, found to be no more alarming than rust.

However, once such a theory had been formulated and expressed, it persisted. Mutiny at sea followed by complete mystery as to what became of mutineers and victims was too tantalizing a story to be discarded readily. Although it has generally been considered as convincingly disproved by other factors and considerations, it nevertheless persisted for a great many years, and there are still books available where the mutiny theory is upheld by the writer and claimed to be supported by a reasonable assessment of the few known facts.

Possibly an offshoot of the mutiny theory was the claim that the men shipped as crew aboard the *Mary Celeste* were cut-throats from the American eastern seaboard. The story of one of the barrels of raw alcohol being found damaged was good enough to start, at a later date, the rumour that the villainous crew had tampered with the cargo and after becoming drunk on the crude spirit ran amok, murdering the captain and his family. But after such a piece of fabricated villainy there is only silence. The mutiny by a drunken crew theory does not explain what happened to the occupants who launched the *Mary Celeste*'s boat and presumably rowed away from her pitching side.

Even launching that boat was not accomplished without, seemingly, some difficulty, for the deckrail had proved an obstacle, and a part of it had been cut away. The severed section of rail was left lying on the deck. But all that can be said of this detail is that it displays determination to be away from the *Mary Celeste* and does not point to why she was deserted nor where the occupants of the boat hoped to make for.

The fact that Captain Briggs had taken with him, besides his sextant and ship's papers, his ship's chronometer and navigation book suggests that he had hopes of successfully voyaging in the small boat towards the known sea lanes, his one hope of being picked up in the Atlantic in December.

The *Dei Gratia* sailed into the harbour at Gibraltar in the evening of December 12th. The *Mary Celeste*, with Deveau at the helm, arrived some hours later, on the morning of the 13th, to be welcomed by a curious crowd of spectators who watched her drop anchor as though she were a ghost ship. Already the story of her being found deserted was common knowledge on the Rock, and the authorities were making the first moves to set up a court of inquiry.

The salvage court ultimately awarded Captain Moorhouse and the *Dei Gratia's* crew the sum of seventeen hundred pounds for salvaging the deserted *Mary Celeste* and bringing her to port. A curious figure. It amounted to a pound for each barrel of commercial alcohol in the *Mary Celeste's* holds.

From the western side of the Atlantic came James Winchester to take possession of the salvaged brigantine. He was the chief owner, and he was able to tell those directly interested in solving the mystery of the deserted ship that Benjamin Briggs, whom he had known for a good many years, was a ship's master who allowed no drinking of intoxicants aboard his vessel.

He had an interview with David Moorhouse, whose reputation as a ship's master was known to him. He spoke to Deveau and various members of the *Dei Gratia's* crew who had been aboard the *Mary Celeste*. He inspected the vessel himself.

As a result of his questions and the answers they had received, and of his own search and examination of the ship, he readily gave his own considered view of what had happened.

In James Winchester's view a rough sea had shifted the cargo. At least one barrel had been damaged sufficiently to release alcohol fumes that blew off the hatch cover after the pressure had built up. This happened not a great while before the *Dei Gratia* came up with the abandoned brigantine. He felt that the unrusted state of several razors left behind by the crew as well as some of their clothing hung up to dry supported this argument, and it was one with which Captain Moorhouse was in full agreement.

According to the Winchester explanation of what most likely happened, Captain Briggs, with a wife and small child aboard, became alarmed by the fumes rising from the hold with the blown hatch cover, and feared for the lives of all aboard and in his charge. He gave the order to abandon ship without loss of time, fearing a possible explosion in the hold and not knowing fully the actual amount of damage suffered by the cargo.

So the ship's boat was launched and stood off, its occupants expecting to see the ship they had left blown skywards, for there was a fire in the galley by which the cook heated meals, and at any moment the fumes might reach the galley.

However, no further explosion occurred, and when a breeze blew up and freshened Benjamin Briggs most likely decided that the fumes were being blown away, and had ordered his men to row back to the *Mary Celeste*.

Unfortunately the breeze continued to freshen, and the deserted brigantine had enough canvas on her rigging to ensure she moved smartly before it. The men in the small boat could not overtake her. Indeed, they had to row with a growing feeling of despair as the realization came to them that not only would they fail to reach their abandoned ship, but that the seas were rising under the whip of the wind, which at that time of the year would have been bitterly cold.

In the view of James Winchester the ten lives in the small boat had been lost when the men's strength gave out and the seas began to pound it without mercy.

This is the general consensus of responsible opinion today. But even at the time it was first made scores of incredible rumours and theories were being circulated both in Europe and North America. The story of possible mutiny was believed by many, although there was nothing known to support it save the rusty cutlass left on deck and some alleged damage to the *Mary Celeste*'s bows. However, this last point was one that was argued hotly, for seamen who had gone aboard the *Mary Celeste* in

Gibraltar had claimed the damage was no more than normal wear and tear due to port dockings and facing heavy seas. In short, the bow timbers had been strained, and from understandable hazards. They had not been damaged in a scuffle aboard.

Or even deliberately.

It was no less a person than the Queen's Advocate at Gibraltar, a gentleman of lively imagination named Flood, who suggested that the crew might have wantonly damaged the ship they were deserting to make her appear not worth salvaging – in short, a floating wreck that could be left to tide and time to dismantle and disintegrate. Mr. Flood had a reason for purporting to think the way he did. This was his involvement with the terms of the claim for salvage. In no sense was he completely disinterested in weighing the probabilities of what had happened. He was one who believed a drunken crew had got clamorous for blood and had murdered their mate and captain as well as the captain's wife and child. After throwing their victims overboard they had fled in the brigantine's only boat.

Not only was this general argument unsupported by anything of weight, but the marine surveyor at Gibraltar, who spent five hours and more examining the salvaged *Mary Celeste,* had neither claimed the cargo had been damaged wantonly nor charged that damage had been deliberately done to the ship.

Possibly the Queen's Advocate's sensational suggestion was in some measure responsible for an even more sensational suggestion that was made a short while subsequently. This was to the effect that Benjamin Briggs was responsible for the mystery.

The captain of the *Mary Celeste,* it was suggested, had gone out of his mind. A madman had committed murder and mayhem aboard the ill-fated craft.

While this was certainly in the tradition of some of the best horror fiction of the period, it was, as a valid claim, so far-fetched as to be untenable. Benjamin Briggs was supposedly a religious maniac, although he had never paraded himself as a particularly devout man. But he was overcome by a compulsive obsession, comparable to that of the notorious Captain Ahab of

Moby Dick. In his case it was a determination to remove those he loved and those in his charge from the sinful snares of the world and its fleshpots.

His mind deranged in this way, he had seized the cutlass that had been found and killed his wife and his little daughter. Stimulated by this fearful blood-letting, he had stalked his mate and the other members of the brigantine's crew. With the cunning of a homicidal maniac he had cut them down, one by one. Afterwards he had thrown the butchered bodies over the side. Satiation had brought a return of reason, and he had been stricken by what he had done in the time when his mind was demented. He had launched the boat and set himself adrift, bent only on removing himself from a ship he had turned into a slaughter-house.

With this macabre theory there was no attempt to explain how a madman had succeeded in defeating seven members of his crew, who might have been expected to notice the coming of insanity in their captain. Nor was the absence of fearful blood-stains explained.

A number of proponents of this blood-reeking high seas drama had a variant. They insisted that the remorse-ridden murderer had thrown himself from the deck of his own ship without pondering to consider, in that case, who could have launched the missing boat.

The *Dei Gratia*'s first officer gave his own version of what could have happened, just as he had explained it to Captain Moorhouse after returning shaken from clambering aboard the deserted *Mary Celeste*.

To the more rational-minded at the court of inquiry it seemed then, as now, that the storm that had sent some of the barrels rolling around in the hold, and had damaged one sufficiently to make it leak, might have sprung a timber out of true; thus enough seawater could have been let in, while the waves were high, to collect to a depth of three feet. When the storm gave over, the gaping timber was squeezed back in alignment and no more seawater was shipped in calmer weather. Whether

Captain Briggs gave the order to abandon ship because of the evidence of a leak, or because the hatch cover was blown off by alcohol fumes, or for possibly both these reasons, is still the point from which different opinions branch.

But whatever the captain's reason, it is certain that his crew were behaving in an orderly manner when they abandoned ship, and there is every likelihood that they were obeying their captain's command, given because he had the wellbeing of all aboard the *Mary Celeste* very much at heart. This would have been consistent with Benjamin Briggs' known character. He was a respected ship's captain and a mariner of great experience. He would not have acted in anything amounting to panic. He may have been urging haste, but he would have thought out his course of action and would have been taking it because it seemed to him the wisest and best to be taken in the circumstances as he understood them.

So the laden boat pulled away from a ship that was not doomed, leaving behind a mystery still debated as it has been from the time of the Gibraltar court of inquiry.

Perhaps it was to be expected that a number of alleged survivors should turn up around the globe from time to time in the years following. These undoubted impostors were responsible for some of the more bizarre fables put in circulation about what happened that winter's day when the boat dropped over the *Mary Celeste*'s side, leaving the brigantine to drift into the path of the approaching *Dei Gratia*.

It is certain the small boat with any survivors was not to be seen through David Moorhouse's telescope or Benjamin Briggs' friend would have turned his ship around and sailed after it. Without first sighting that open boat it would have been futile to go seeking it with no clue to the direction in which it had gone. This despite the fact that the *Dei Gratia*'s captain had formed the firm opinion that the boat had left the *Mary Celeste* not very long before his first officer clambered aboard the deserted brigantine.

After James Winchester had taken possession of the *Mary*

Celeste she was refitted and put back into the trade for which she had been built. She continued to ply the high seas, carrying cargoes up and down the Atlantic, for another thirteen years, until she piled up on Roshell's Reef, off the coast of Haiti, the voodoo island, on January 3rd, 1885.

When she sank under the Caribbean waves she left in nautical history a name associated with what is possibly the most famous of all mysteries of the sea.

6

The Princes in the Tower

For nearly four hundred years millions of eyes have grown moist when reading the soliloquy by Tyrell which opens Act IV, Scene III, of Shakespeare's *Richard III*.

But there is at least the likelihood that those millions of tears have been invoked for the wrong reason, and all the anger against Richard for having his young nephews murdered may have been unjustified. Richard Crookback may have been innocent.

Whether he was guilty or innocent is still a mystery, as is the question of who was guilty. The two pathetic youngsters, one a King of England and the other his younger brother, died violently in the Tower of London. Of that there is no historical doubt. Such doubts as exist relate to when they died and who, in fact, benefited from their death.

When Shakespeare began writing "The tyrannous and bloody act is done" he was either recording a colourful version of history, or else he was furthering the dissemination of a piece of deliberate fiction begun by Henry VII a century before and given support as fact by all the Tudors and their most fervent adherents.

If this last is indeed true, as a good many modern researchers and students of the later fifteenth century believe, then the death of the young sons of Edward IV in the Tower of London has still to be convincingly explained.

Unfortunately any explanation provided hitherto tends to be partisan, depending on how the writer views the characters of two kings, the hunchback Richard of Gloucester, who has more often than not been accorded less than his due for what he achieved during his uneasy years of kingship, and Henry Tudor, the Welshman with a mistrust of the English, who was as much an opportunist as his royal opponent who died on Bosworth Field and very possibly was even more ruthless, but better at concealing it.

One must face the uncomfortable fact that, when describing the thirteen-year-old Edward V and his younger brother Richard, Duke of York, being smothered while they slept with a prayer-book on their pillow, Shakespeare might have been lending himself to the business of penning Tudor propaganda.

They were more likely to have been slain with a sword, and if Miles Forest was one of the slayers, the other was very possibly Black Will Slater, not a companion named Dighton. But even this much depends upon a confession supposedly made by Sir James Tyrell – as he preferred to spell his name – at the time of his execution, seventeen years after Henry Tudor won the English throne for himself.

Indeed, the mystery becomes more involved as one considers the various interests concerned. But today, as any reader of crime stories understands and knows, a great store is set by motivation in any narrative dealing with a murder. When the motivation in the murder of the Princes in the Tower is considered, one finds little in the case of Richard of Gloucester, but rather a surprising amount in the case of Henry Tudor.

To be clear in this matter of motivation in the crime one must appreciate how the historical pieces fitted in the jigsaw puzzle of Lancastrians and Yorkists at the time of the Wars of the Roses.

Edward IV, the father of the murdered Princes in the Tower, was a Yorkist. He was born in Rouen, in Normandy, which was then an English possession. In 1460, when he was twenty-two, he became the Yorkist leader and at the battle of Mortimer's Cross, in Herefordshire, he won a signal victory over the Lancastrian forces. Upon his return to London he was proclaimed king.

However, the times were not only unsettled, but saw many changes in the fortunes of both sides engaged in the struggle between the white rose of York and the red rose of Lancaster.

Edward won another victory at Towton, but then his star shone less brightly. The joining of forces by Clarence and Warwick and their determined array when they marched against him, disheartened his followers. Before he could gamble on winning another victory six thousand of them plucked the white rose emblem from their jerkins and deserted.

Edward IV was suddenly a king without the men and arms necessary to defend his kingdom. He rode for the coast and went aboard a ship that hoisted sail and took him to Holland.

Although he had turned tail, he was not a quitter. In the Netherlands he spent his time in intrigue and making arrangements for a return to take up the fight against the Lancastrians, who were in power at the moment.

When he had the army he required he sailed back to England. Perhaps it was just as well for his comfort of mind that on the voyage he had no inkling that one day his daughter Elizabeth would marry the son of Edmund Tudor, Earl of Richmond, after her husband Henry had finally crushed the white rose at Bosworth. Edmund Tudor's father was Owen Tudor of Angelsey, who had married Queen Catherine, the widow of the warrior king Henry V. Edmund himself married Margaret Beaufort, who was a descendant of another warrior king, Edward III, through John of Gaunt.

There was thus plenty of royal blood in opposition in the Wars of the Roses. It stemmed from different directions making harsh rivals of those through whose veins it flowed. This fact was well appreciated by the shrewd Henry Tudor, who had been brought up in France. After winning the Battle of Bosworth and marrying Elizabeth, he doffed the red rose of Lancaster as his emblem and wore, instead, the freshly conceived Tudor rose, which was a heraldic combination of both the red rose of Lancaster and the white rose of York.

No longer was royal blood to come from rival factions and different directions. The Tudors established a monopoly and defeated any who challenged it.

But earlier, when Edward IV and his men-at-arms from the

Continent headed inland from the sea, after landing what was really an invasion force, history was still to be made on the battlefield, and two important battles left Edward the victor by weight of arms.

The first of these trials of strength was the battle of Barnet and the second was the decisive victory for Yorkist arms at Tewkesbury. In both battles the Burgundians who had marched with Edward proved staunch allies of the English king they recognized. As a result of these hard-fought actions the Lancastrian Henry VI and the powerful Earl of Warwick, nicknamed the king-maker, were no longer powers for Edward to reckon with. Both had been slain.

The white rose of York was really blooming in a brief period of high summer.

The summer was to end with violent storms.

These began the day Edward IV died. That day was April 9th, 1483.

The son who was to succeed to the throne Edward IV had made secure was a pale-faced youngster of thirteen who had been given his father's name. His mother, the rather tearful and fearful Elizabeth Woodville, was not a woman with any sort of will of her own. When she found herself a widow she sought advice in almost everything she did from her brother-in-law, the hunchback Duke of Gloucester, who was ambitious and suddenly aware that a throne might be within his reach.

Edward V, the boy-king, had been born in Westminster on November 3rd, 1470, the very year his father fled to the Netherlands and made his way to Burgundy. By no rating could this be considered a hopeful beginning.

Certainly when he became king, upon the death of his warrior father, he was hardly ready for embarking on his duties of a monarch. Like his mother, he looked to his Uncle Richard for help and guidance.

Richard was quite prepared to run the country as Protector during the remaining years of young Edward's minority, but he was fully aware that those years would be a testing time. A boy-king as the head of State would be an open invitation for the Lancastrians to return for another trial of strength. Richard, in his own interest and possibly in the interest of Edward IV's sons, had the youthful king and his brother, the Duke of York, sent to the royal apartments that were maintained at that time in the Tower of London, which was not a prison, but a fortress that could be defended against attacking enemies.

So we see that the picture so usually presented of the Princes in the Tower being uncomfortably housed prisoners is false. The Tower of London at that period, apart from its purely military value as a citadel of the English capital, can reasonably be considered as an annexe to the royal palace at Westminster, where the elder prince had first seen the light of day in the Sanctuary.

Richard was induced to be inward-looking by the state of the country when he took it over.

His brother Edward had sometimes been too ready to ride into battle, and upon occasion he had found that courage did not compensate for military strength and inexpert tactics. Although he had suffered reverses in England, he had succeeded in recovering his grasp on a crown that had temporarily slipped from him after his success at Towton Field. But his ventures across the narrow seas in France had been less inspired. Despite the harsh measures he took to gain men and supplies, his endeavours to regain lost English possessions across the Channel had no happy outcome in the military field. The only compensations were the trade treaties with Continental merchants which he was able to arrange; these were valuable to English merchants at home and were to have greater value in the future.

Richard was not really concerned with relationships abroad. His idea of ruling was to rule the English, as the Tudors, who did not live in England, understood very well. True, he tended to become obsessed with what potential enemies might achieve in plotting behind his hunched back, but any understanding of his character must take into account the effect of his physical deformity. It was an age when princes of royal blood were prone to act as tyrants and to take out insurance for the future by hiring the services of assassins. Thereafter the assassins had to be disposed of to silence any tongues inclined towards looseness.

Such was the practising precept of the times throughout Europe. It became, indeed, a code of behaviour. Francis Bacon wrote more than a century after the white rose had withered, "It is a miserable state of mind, to have few things to desire, and many things to fear : and yet that commonly is the case of kings". That typical Baconian aphorism seems to sum up the state of mind that must have been Richard Crookback's when he decided to cease being Protector and assume the crown so that he could rule the country in his own right.

However, what was his right has been something that has been warmly debated for half a millennium.

Richard mounted the throne under a cloud, and certainly the circumstances were not only peculiar, but sinister to even the most casual glance. Certainly the glance thrown in his direction by the exiled Henry Tudor, no longer entitled to call himself the Earl of Richmond after his father, who had died under the headsman's axe, was anything but casual. In the exiled Tudor, and leader of what remained at that time of the Lancastrian cause and pretensions, burned a fierce and consuming ambition as well as a grim desire for revenge on the House of York.

Richard's gamble on hiding his fears and his hump under the crown of an anointed king was unquestionably considered by the exiled Tudor to be a personal challenge. From that moment the issue was joined. It was an issue that could only end in a warlike confrontation, and Henry Tudor, with his Welsh wits serving him well, decided to pick the time.

That would come, he decided, when he had given the crippled upstart Richard III a period for stewing in his own unsavoury juice. Richard, he shrewdly anticipated, would take all the measures necessary to make himself unpopular with the nobles and the common people.

The image, as might be said today, of Richard was one that

Richard could and would do little to improve in the eyes of his subjects.

Time, in short, was on the side of Henry Tudor.

It was certainly not on the side of the Princes who were still living in the Tower's royal apartments. So far as Richard was concerned, it was a case of out of sight, out of mind. He had a formal announcement made that the two youngsters had died in the Tower.

No more. They had died.

Of course the country was shocked. At once rumours began to circulate. One was that Richard had had the boys murdered, most conveniently for his ambition to become king in young Edward's stead.

A bygone rumour also circulated again, for it seemed in keeping with the fresh ones. This was to the effect that Richard had been responsible, years before, for the drowning of the Duke of Clarence in a butt of Malmsey wine. Richard had been able to do little about refuting that rumour, which began its widening ripples in February 1478, the month Clarence died, except protest at the way Clarence had ended his life, as he had protested earlier at Clarence's attainder and being condemned to death for his intrigues against brother Edward.

Not that Richard's protest at the time had weighed with his brother, the King, with whom he was on the best of terms. Possibly this was why whoever was responsible for Clarence's death chose a moment to bring it about when Richard was out of London, most likely in the North of England.

Now, on July 6th, 1483, the rumour was alive again in the start of an historic smear campaign that has few equals. This was the day Richard became King of England.

The smear quickly widened in the distrustful climate of the new and very ill-starred reign for the House of York.

For instance, apart from the mysterious death of the young Edward V and his brother, Richard's own actions appeared on the surface to be inconsistent except for a man who had been determined to seize the crown at all costs to anyone save himself.

It was remembered that when his brother, Edward IV, died suddenly, still a comparatively young man of forty, Richard was somewhere along the Scottish border. As soon as he received the news of Edward's death he hastened south as far as York, where he attended a Requiem Mass for the dead monarch's soul and afterwards had his nephew Edward, then staying with his uncle Lord Rivers in Ludlow Castle, proclaimed the new king, Edward V.

Richard had immediately taken a solemn oath to support the boy-king and render him full allegiance and a subject's devotion.

Now, three months later, with the crown on his own head, the rumours hinted that Richard's prompt action after his brother's death was no more than a device to make Lord Rivers give up his charge and send the new king to the capital to be crowned. Moreover, it would get Edward out of the care of his mother's family, for the Woodvilles, who had been given prestige, as well as wealth and rank, by the new king's father, presented to Richard of Gloucester a power he wished to have quickly quenched.

In actual fact, Lord Rivers had his own reasons for rushing young Edward to London and getting him crowned. He wished to gather the Woodvilles around him and call a council of State that would make sure Richard gained no control over the boy-king. Actually such an action was against the terms of the will left by Edward IV, for in that document the late king had shown clearly the high regard in which he held his brother Richard of Gloucester by naming him as the guardian responsible for his two young sons.

In the event two columns of fighting men started for London. From Shropshire and the Welsh border marched Lord Rivers' retainers, six thousand in number, armed and ready for action if the word was given. In their midst, rather scared by the display of might and his uncle's determination to lose no time in reaching London, was young Edward. It is very doubtful whether the boy felt that he was a king or considered that the noisy soldiers trudging the rutted roads leading east were really his subjects. He probably understood nothing of what was involved in a play of what we could look upon as power politics of a simple, explosive kind.

South from York came Richard, with only six hundred retainers. None of them was accoutred as a soldier. All wore heavy bands of black and appeared to be dressed for mourning. At least, when they set out. Doubtless the typical rains of an English April soon left them looking moist and bedraggled.

Rivers and his small army won the race and the first orders were given for calling a council of State. Richard was not mentioned. The Woodville faction, it has been claimed, were actually plotting to have Richard assassinated. If so, it was a desperately bad example to set a man who could do his own thinking and learn from his personal enemies' mistakes. A cousin of Richard's, the Duke of Buckingham, found himself torn between two possible allegiances and after debating the likely outcome of a military showdown at this time decided he had best place himself at Richard's side. He mounted a swift horse and rode north to meet Richard, who was taking his time on the journey south. However, when Buckingham informed him of what was being planned by Lord Rivers and the Woodville faction Richard bestirred himself. His men stopped looking like drowned rats and became soldiers, and glad at the change.

Indeed, they appeared so formidable when they arrived at Stony Stratford and confronted the force Lord Rivers was bringing northwards that Richard, acting like a commander, had the other leader seized, whereupon Rivers' men turned their coats and joined Richard's forces.

Lord Rivers was sent under armed guard to Yorkshire, where he was kept a prisoner in a royal castle and away from the Woodvilles in the south. Richard felt he had drawn the sharpest of his enemies' fangs.

He marched his men into London, and appeared at their

head on May 4th, less than a month after the death of his brother, which had been entirely unsuspected. Indeed, had it been generally known that Edward had been close to dying, there is almost no chance that his young heir would have been allowed to remain in Ludlow.

Young Edward and his brother were now in the charge of Uncle Richard, as their father had decided in his will. Their mother, with the Woodvilles in acute disorder after Lord Rivers' capture, turned to her brother-in-law for help and guidance. Richard gave her one ear while listening to other voices at the same time. He put the Princes in the Bishop's palace at St. Paul's.

Richard was a busy man during the days he stayed with his mother at Baynard's Castle. Just over a week after he arrived back in London, Parliament was summoned to meet on the 25th of the following month. That would be three days after the coronation of young Edward, on June 22nd.

Orders were given for the new king's sumptuous coronation robes to be made.

There was a great deal of bustling commotion in preparing for immediately future events, and then the Bishop of Bath and Wells threw an episcopal spanner in the royal works, by announcing that at the time of Edward IV's marriage to Elizabeth Woodville he was already married in the eyes of the Church to the Lady Eleanor Talbot, a daughter of the Earl of Shrewsbury. He had been a witness to the earlier ceremony and he produced documents that confirmed his claim. The bishop, Dr. Stillington, had succeeded in proclaiming that the royal sons of Edward IV were illegitimate.

In effect, Edward V was not entitled to wear the crown of England. This had been a State secret Edward IV had not shared with his brother. Lady Eleanor Talbot had entered a convent when her husband turned from her to Elizabeth Woodville. She had died in 1466.

It has been claimed that this secret may have been the reason for the curious assassination of Clarence.

Now the marriage was a secret no longer, Richard viewed Lord Rivers' hurry to reach London with his nephew in a very different light. He set himself to defeat a group of conspirators who had tried to use events for their own benefit. Lord Hastings was arrested and executed. Instead of executing another of the Woodville faction, Cardinal Morton, he merely banished him to an estate in Wales.

This act of clemency was to cost him dear.

Meanwhile Parliament debated this complex state of affairs and decided that Prince Edward could not be crowned because he was an illegitimate son. The rightful heir to the throne was his Uncle Richard.

But the news that the Princes had died in the Tower removed doubts from the minds of any who may have thought Richard was entering his kingdom by a secret back door. Or, rather, that was how it appeared. If the proclaimed Edward V was dead, then there was no obstacle to Richard ascending the throne.

If, in such circumstances, Richard connived at the murder of the Princes in the Tower, what was his purpose? Parliament had already cleared the path to throne and crown for him. If he had their deaths announced merely as a matter of expediency, to leave the Woodville faction nothing on which to build their hopes of rebellion against his rule, then he was at worst guilty of being a liar and throwing dust in the eyes of his bemused subjects. But he probably thought a lie was justified. After all, his brother Edward's married life had been a lie that had served its own purpose until his death.

Richard went to his coronation feeling confident that he had acted for the best.

Within a short while uglier rumours were spreading throughout the land about him. He was claimed to have poisoned his wife, Anne, so that he could propose marriage to his niece Elizabeth. Later, Elizabeth married Henry Tudor, and so justified the creation of his new Tudor rose out of the former opposed blooms. He was supposed to have steeped his royal hands in the blood of numerous opponents who might have challenged him. But the evidence, when examined, is slight, and nearly all in Richard's favour.

History, it seems, has dealt unkindly with Richard Crookback's memory, which is largely the fault of the historians, especially those who accepted without too close examination the evidence offered by his successors and detractors, the Tudors.

Yet as a statesman Richard III claims appreciative recognition by Englishmen as the first instigator of a postal system as well as a system of bail for arrested prisoners. He even insisted that the country's laws should be translated into English and thereafter retained in the native tongue.

He was a patron of the new magic of the printed word, for when Caxton set up his press in Westminster the printer received marked signs of the royal approval, and in return he dedicated one of his works to Richard.

"My redoubted lord and king," was Caxton's description of his patron.

Possibly because there had been so many changes during the Wars of the Roses in coats of arms and escutcheons, Richard became responsible for founding and establishing the College of Heralds. It is still today a memorial to his foresight and love of order.

However, his aptitude for rule was not to be left for long unchallenged. Unrelenting and unforgiving rebels like Morton soon joined forces to plot rebellion, and a lead was given to them by Henry Tudor, who was waiting in the wings for the right moment to step into the centre of the stage. If the illegitimate Edward V was a king, at least in name, for a mere two months and thirteen days, his Uncle Richard was a crowned monarch for only two years and forty-seven days.

Richard had to take his army into the flat fields of Leicestershire to meet the Earl of Richmond and his men who were prepared to risk their lives to make him Henry VII. The white rose and red met in a conflict which, apart from some later risings which were abortive, was the final and conclusive battle of that pitiless civil war that had drained Plantagenet blood.

The last desperate round was fought at Bosworth. First Richard lost his horse and then his life.

Henry Tudor came to London and was crowned. He was a greedy man with a liking for ships. He accumulated a great treasure for his family, for he felt they had been too long in the wilderness and wanted vigorous sustenance against any possible ill-wind that might bring them misfortune. Having ensured riches on earth, he gave his mind to riches in heaven, and he had built the Gothic lady chapel in Westminster Abbey, which was in 1509 to become his last resting-place.

There was something else Henry Tudor did.

He set about tearing to pieces any reputation for wise rule gained by his predecessor on the English throne. He was responsible for scribes vilifying Richard's character. What they couldn't prove to Richard's discredit was hinted at, and if hints were not considered strong enough fictions were invented. There was a very good reason for this mischievous denigration of the last English king to die in battle fighting for his crown.

Henry Tudor had no rightful claim to that crown. He had one trumped up through his mother's side of the family, and he was careful to marry the Yorkist Princess Elizabeth, sister of the dead Princes in the Tower, but it was a manoeuvre to still tongues that might become clamorous after minds had been given time to think past the fog of Bosworth's disaster for the House of York.

It was imperative that the coming of Henry Tudor should appear to be in the nature of a rescue operation to the bulk of Englishmen, who were thoroughly sick of civil war and the hard times it brought to husbandman and burgher alike. So Richard became the wicked monarch who had been rightfully slain by the crusading House of Tudor.

Henry paid an Italian scribe named Polydore Virgil to write a history of the times. Into it went all the claims made against Richard's character. They also appeared in works written by Cardinal Morton and Robert Fabyan.

4—FHM * *

So far as these alleged records concern the Princes in the Tower, what was written was purported to be confirmed by a confession supposedly made by Sir James Tyrell before his execution in 1502. Richard was branded as the instigator of the two boys' murder. According to this version Tyrell undertook to have the murders committed when Sir Robert Brackenbury, Governor of the Tower, decided he could not dabble in regicide. Tyrell paid two toughs of the period, Miles Forest and Black Will Slater, to kill the brothers. For this Tyrell supposedly received a shoulder touch with Richard's sword.

It was a poorly invented tale. Tyrell had been made a knight some dozen years or so before the murders. Slater later received cash payments from Henry VII. Bishop Stillington was jailed by Henry, presumably to stop him enlarging on what he knew. Moreover, documents have been discovered which modern historians claim point to one of the murdered Princes being alive only five months before Bosworth was fought. If one was alive at that time, presumably both were, and at that date Richard could have had no sudden reason for murdering them. In that event they were alive and concealed when Henry Tudor became king and set about changing an Act of Parliament that would legitimize the Princess Elizabeth, whom he intended to marry. The same act would have legitimized her brothers. Then, in that case, if they were still alive they were a danger and constant threat to his own security.

Henry took occasion to have many Yorkists imprisoned or executed. He could have ordered the execution of the Princes in the Tower and then paid scribes to ensure the deed was laid at Richard's door.

It is now held by many researchers and historians that the two boys were killed some eleven months after Bosworth was fought, perhaps in July 1486, for it was about this time that Tyrell received a special pardon from Henry. Not only that, but Henry gave Tyrell a governorship some months later that took him out of the country and away from attentive ears. It was Tyrell's bad luck that he again became mixed up in the Yorkist cause and lost his head. In any case, it was a way of silencing him permanently.

At a later date bones were supposedly uncovered in Westminster Abbey that were claimed to be those of the tragic brothers. But the real origin of those bones was never proved. They became merely another fragment in a legend which is still wrapped in mystery.

7

The Mystery of the Diamond Necklace

One famous historical mystery that has captured the imaginations of romantics and novelists is another that concerns the French Court. It centres around the person of the tragic queen, Marie-Antoinette, Austrian born and reared. There have been claims that the diamond necklace she never wore helped to further the cause of the militants who started the political earthquake known to history as the French Revolution.

This is to be doubted.

But certainly the curious sequence of events surrounding the alleged purchase of the necklace and the refusal to pay the agreed price, with clandestine bargaining and secret meetings that involved other persons of rank, did little to show Marie-Antoinette in a good light to her French subjects, who had accepted her arrival among them with strong misgivings.

All of which is a story that created at the time it became generally known a grave scandal that rocked the French Court with a violence felt throughout the nation. Among the echoing rumbles of heady disaffection heard throughout France before the Revolution broke on an unprepared regime the affair of the diamond necklace became just another echo.

It was a double-sounding echo. It not only echoed a Court scandal, but also a profound mystery.

All of it eddied around Marie-Antoinette, and this was really quite unfair. For she, although queen in her adopted land, was treated like a pawn in a game to make money by selling a necklace of which she was ignorant when its price was agreed.

Indeed, the necklace was never intended for her in the first place.

It had been made for the notorious Madame Du Barry. Marie-Antoinette and the Du Barry had only three things in common. They were women, they were both concerned with the most notorious necklace in all history, and they both lost their heads under the guillotine's axe.

They were never friends. Indeed, they took care never to meet. Yet in this strange affair of the necklace their names are linked like those of sisters.

This can be considered another of history's unsavoury ironies.

Louis XV was a rake and a wastrel. He was susceptible to any pair of bright young female eyes that met his questing gaze with anything like a challenge. His subjects, with true Gallic humour, dubbed him Louis the Well-beloved, and so he was by the smiling young women on whom he conferred his royal favours, and poured the contents of the royal treasury. He was a French king with scant love for England, and it was during his reign that Wolfe defeated Montcalm in the hard struggle for supremacy in Canada. The only consolation Louis found after hearing the news was in retiring to Versailles and enjoying the attentions of his female flatterers.

One of the most adept at getting her way with him was a certain redhead. She became his favourite and he gave her a château and a title.

She is known to history as the Comtesse Du Barry, and her château was at Louveciennes, only a short distance from Versailles.

She was born of working-class parents, but once she had caught the roving royal eye she displayed the awareness of a magpie at collecting bright trinkets, especially when they were of great value, and most of those she recived from Louis were of very great value, judged by the standard of living her own family enjoyed.

Louis followed his grandfather, Louis XIV, who had created the mystery of the Man in the Iron Mask, to the throne of France. He was a child at the time, and grew accustomed to others attending to affairs of State while he concentrated on attending to his personal pleasures. It was a habit he never grew out of.

The women who entered his life encouraged him not to change. Madame Jeanne Pompadour carved her own place in the history of France by being his favourite. After her star had set, the Du Barry's rose in the ascendant; and it shone for years with a translucent brightness that made her famous beyond the frontiers of France.

She had not lost her hold over Louis when his unusually long reign ended rather unexpectedly after he had caught smallpox and died despite the best ministrations from the Court physicians and surgeons.

He left a good deal of unfinished business when he breathed his last. One piece was the matter of paying a firm of Paris jewellers for a magnificent diamond necklace they had been creating, purchasing stones of rare quality and matching them to provide an ornament not only of great cost, but of great beauty. Indeed, the necklace was to be an outstanding triumph of the jeweller's art.

Louis had one person in mind for receiving that costly gift as a present from his royal hands—the Comtesse Du Barry.

The firm of jewellers who had been commissioned to find the necessary stones and to create this marvel was the most reputable one of Boehmer and Bassenge. Monsieur Boehmer, the senior partner, took it upon himself personally to tour Europe collecting the stones he required. It has been said that he spent all of five years on this quest before he was satisfied that he had acquired the diamonds necessary to make the necklace he envisioned as suitable for the Du Barry's shapely neck.

The stones he purchased cost the equivalent of several fortunes, and they numbered some six hundred. All were pure unflawed diamonds and large, some of them exceptionally large, and when joined in what was a masterpiece of the jeweller's skill provided a breath-taking sight as they flashed back thousands of brilliant coruscations of light.

Against a pale throat they appeared like a collar of blazing fire. There had been no piece of jewellery previously designed to compare with the Du Barry's necklace. It was a complex creation of pendants and separate strings of diamonds, with looped tassels of the stones that extended over the wearer's shoulders and even draped the back of her neck, while in the centre of the front was a blaze of the finest stones in a giant cluster.

Unfortunately for the Du Barry, although she knew all about the quest to secure the diamonds and the skill being displayed to create her wonderful necklace, she never wore it. She did not even handle it.

Louis caught his dose of smallpox before Monsieur Boehmer could make delivery of the fabulous necklace. Even worse, from the viewpoint of the appalled jeweller, Louis died before he could pay for what he had considered a pretty trinket. The necklace, in the currency of the period, was valued by Boehmer and Bassenge at more than one and a half million livres. Payment would have entailed a deep dip into the country's exchequer. Not that Louis would have been averse. He had been dipping into it all his life, and in fact he could be said to have come close to plundering it to further his royal pleasures. It was another habit he had acquired and not surrendered. If anything, his taste became more expensive the longer he lived, and he was sixty-four when he died.

He had been thirty when the Du Barry was born.

With the king dead the redhead had to continue to think for herself, which she was very capable of doing, but this time without a royal protector. She retired to her château and from a window watched another Louis come to the throne and face the unpopularity earned for him by his expensive predecessor.

Monsieur Boehmer knew there was no chance of taking his necklace to the new king. It seemed his one hope was to make overtures to the Du Barry. She was rich—she had seen to that. But she did not forget that she had come from humble beginnings, and she knew the value of a sou as well as a livre. For Louis XV to give her the necklace costing a million and a half livres was one thing. She would accept it graciously and gracefully. But for her to find the price of such an article was quite something else. She already had caskets of jewels, and she lived in a perpetual pink haze, surrounded by tapestries and furnishings and china of that dusky rose colour that has become known to the world as her own creation, and for that reason is still, nearly two centuries later, called rose Du Barry whenever it is displayed.

She informed Monsieur Boehmer that, while she appreciated all the time and effort that had gone into his masterpiece in diamonds, she had no wish to buy it from him.

Monsieur Boehmer could not help but feel rebuffed. He regretted that Madame Du Barry was not of noble birth. True aristocrats might have felt an obligation to pay for something originally intended for them. It was part of the ancient understanding of *noblesse oblige,* the code by which they lived.

However, Madame Du Barry had none of the sensitivity of a person of gentle birth, and this was a fact of life Monsieur Boehmer had to regret. He locked his masterpiece in diamonds away in a safe and looked around for anyone who could be considered a likely customer. He knew very well there were not many such in the whole of France.

In fact, it may be that he found the only one.

All the same, it did not prove to be a good choice eventually. Fortunately for the harrassed jeweller who was hard pressed for funds and desperately needing a sale for his necklace he could not see into the future.

In the year Louis XV died, 1774, the Cardinal de Rohan had been recalled from Vienna in disgrace, and he returned to France to find that he was very much out of favour with Marie-Antoinette. He tried in the next few years, while Monsieur Boehmer was hunting for a customer for his necklace, to become reconciled to the new Queen of France, for he realized that only in this way could he advance his career. The new king, Louis XVI, was a man who seldom could make up his mind about anything when he could leave the task to someone else, in particular his Austrian wife, who was endeavouring, it seemed, to make Paris the gayest capital in Europe. She enjoyed being a queen, just as she enjoyed going to Versailles and playing at being a shepherdess and sampling the bucolic life.

The Du Barry never joined her. Such games were not her taste. She had known all she wanted to know about the simple life preached by the philosophers Rousseau and Voltaire when she was a young girl and had no wish to return to it even in play.

Not that Rousseau and Voltaire influenced either Marie-Antoinette or the Du Barry, but they managed to die in the same year, which was in the nature of a tidy performance after a pair of lives that were at times inclined towards the untidy, and that year was 1778.

Louis was still leaving things to his wife, while his wife was playing pastoral charades with lambs someone had washed for her, and Monsieur Boehmer was still seeking a customer with a fortune to spare on a magnificent frivolity. And of course the Cardinal de Rohan was still endeavouring without success to get back into the Queen's good graces after being kept from inner Court circles and living in what he considered a provincial wilderness. The past four years he deemed devoted to a cause he refused to believe was hopeless.

He spent another six years trying to bring himself to Marie-Antoinette's notice in a light that would show him to advantage. However, the Austrian spouse of Louis XVI was not to be beguiled by a churchman she judged to be profligate and a man not to be trusted.

Indeed, there is little that can be said in the cardinal's favour, for he was a man who, for one of his calling, thought too highly of the world's fleshpots and took far too much pleasure in purely worldly delights. But the tradesmen of Paris had time for de Rohan. The one thing they found very much in his favour was that he could amply afford to pay for his pleasures. He was a wealthy man.

So, in his way, he was fair game for the unscrupulous. This was amply demonstrated when he became embroiled in the affair of the diamond necklace that Monsieur Boehmer still had on his unhappy hands.

All that the Cardinal de Rohan represented to the jeweller was a likely customer for the notorious strings of diamonds. But Monsieur Boehmer would not have thought of selling the necklace to a cardinal had it not been for a certain woman of the Court who had a quick tongue, taking ways, and an inventive mind.

Her name was Jeanne de Saint-Rémy de Valois, or so she claimed. It sounded imposing. Her married name was even more imposing. It was the Comtesse de Lamotte. Few except the social climber she had married knew that the count was merely a self-styled nobleman. He had elevated himself to the aristocracy without a blush. All the blushes in that family were done by Jeanne, and she was a past-mistress at employing them when it suited her.

She used them in the year 1784 with great effect on the Cardinal de Rohan. The month was March, and cold winds were blowing across the Seine. She came into his life and brought a new warmth. Also hope.

For she told him that she was friendly with Marie-Antoinette, who was always ready to receive her with kindness. That was enough for the cardinal's ears. He told his new friend how much he wished to get back into Marie-Antoinette's favour.

"If only you could help me, I would be so eternally grateful," he told her, in the tone of one begging for a favour.

Jeanne considered the chances in silence, or, rather, she appeared to consider them. She had no access to Marie-Antoinette, but her nimble mind was already working at a scheme that would relieve the cardinal of some of his surplus wealth.

"I may be able to," she said at last. "You must trust me."

De Rohan asked nothing better. He had no one else he could trust.

He would have been perturbed had he known that, a short while later, the *soi-disant* Comte de Lamotte and his lovely countess were putting their heads together. Both had heard of the necklace reposing in the safe of Boehmer and Bassenge.

"We may find Monsieur Boehmer a customer," the count mused happily. "But first you will have to convince the cardinal that the Queen is softening towards him."

He didn't have to spell out the plot that would be used to procure the famous necklace. De Rohan would be a mere pawn in a swindle.

From that time Jeanne brought the cardinal words of encouragement supposedly uttered by Marie-Antoinette. After words of mouth came briefly penned missives, which were just as bogus. But the cardinal, believing that his exceptional patience had been rewarded, felt intoxicated with happiness. It was a state Jeanne did not allow to change, for she brought other letters which sounded more than just friendly.

The Cardinal de Rohan, reading them over in the privacy of his chamber, came to believe that Marie-Antoinette had not only restored him to her favour, but was actually attracted to him as a man.

This mock-intrigue continued through the summer, with the Comtesse de Lamotte carrying amorous letters to and fro between these two most unlikely lovers. Needless to say, Marie-Antoinette knew nothing of the plot being worked out by the unscrupulous charlatans. But a discreet word of what was going on in secret was leaked to Monsieur Boehmer, who made it his business to meet the countess, also in secret. She said it was possible that the cardinal might wish to purchase the diamond necklace to show his personal esteem for a certain lady, and agreed that she could bring the matter of the necklace to his attention.

Monsieur Boehmer may have known more about the countess than she imagined. Anyway, he shrewdly offered her a sizable bribe to start some necessary wheels turning. The sum mentioned was a thousand louis if the necklace was purchased.

The next move in an incredible game of duplicity and deception was Jeanne's going to the cardinal and telling him that she

had something very special to tell him. She had learned that
Marie-Antoinette had expressed a wish that was not intended to
be overheard.

She would love to possess the necklace all Paris knew Monsieur Boehmer had created and not yet sold.

"She shall have it," said the delighted cardinal.

The first negotiations were begun, still in secret, with the firm
of jewellers. The bargaining took some time to complete, for
even the wealthy de Rohan could not raise the total sum
required in payment for the necklace without having to sell
some of his properties. It was at last agreed, however, that he
should purchase the six hundred diamonds in the necklace for
the sum of one million six hundred thousand livres, on condition
that he would be allowed to pay the purchase price in a series of
instalments.

To keep these negotiations moving towards the necklace
changing hands, the countess claimed to have hinted at what
was being arranged to Marie-Antoinette, who now wished to
meet the cardinal in secret.

Had the cardinal not been incredibly gullible for such a man
of the world the married pair of rogues who were planning the
moves would never have been successful with their next imper-
tinent trick.

The cardinal was told an assignation in secret had been
arranged. He was to meet the Queen in the garden at Versailles.
She would be veiled, but even so she was risking much for the
affection she bore him.

De Rohan went to keep the clandestine appointment. He took
a rose. It was a rather conventional token, but, had he stopped
to realize it, he was playing a not unconventional part—at least
it would have been for a man not entitled to wear a cardinal's
red robes and a cardinal's ring.

He was met by a veiled woman who was about Marie-
Antoinette's height and build. When she spoke in a muffled tone
she said the words he wanted to hear.

"I shall forget the past," she murmured behind her veil as she held his rose.

De Rohan would have been shocked and angry had he known that the woman masquerading as the Queen of France keeping an illicit tryst was, although named Marie, a young female of somewhat dubious reputation whose surname was Laguay. She was acting the part for a modest share of some money de Rohan had given Jeanne. She had also been promised that nothing could go wrong with the trick that was being played on the cardinal.

It was a promise that was kept until Monsieur Boehmer decided the transaction had better be covered and made seemly for all their sakes. At least, the suggestion of having Marie-Antoinette's authority for a purchase of the necklace on her behalf is supposed to have come from him. However, much of the manoeuvring in which the various characters in this extremely dangerous and expensive shadow play were involved has to be deduced from the few facts released later, when the entire affair became a first-class Court scandal and was hushed up with an air of all-pervading mystery.

The mystery concerns Marie-Antoinette. Her detractors said later that she was a party to the sale of the necklace, and that she wrote a letter to the Cardinal de Rohan in terms that authorized him to negotiate the purchase on her behalf.

Marie-Antoinette indignantly denounced the claims of her detractors as lies. She said she knew nothing of the transaction undertaken with herself in mind as the recipient of the necklace. Because she was queen her version was accepted—at the time.

What happened was that Monsieur Boehmer was shown a letter allegedly written by Marie-Antoinette. It approved the cardinal's acting on her behalf. It is to be doubted whether the jeweller knew the Queen's handwriting. As for the cardinal, he merely knew it was brought from Marie-Antoinette by the ever-helpful Jeanne, who had even been on hand in the Grove of Venus at Versailles to warn the pair meeting for the first time that someone was approaching. Her interruption with such a

warning was most opportune, for it came at a moment when the
cardinal seemed to be pressing his luck a trifle hard and might
at any instant have the precautionary veil removed.

That would have spelled disaster. De Rohan might be fooled
about Marie-Antoinette's handwriting, and even her voice. But
he knew her face very well.

The cardinal left the premises of the jewellers with the necklace. He arrived with it at the home of the Comte de Lamotte,
where he was introduced to a man who said he was a confiden-
tial valet of the Queen's. When the cardinal left he had passed
the necklace to the man he believed had come from the Queen
to receive it.

He now believed he was in a position to expect signs of royal
favour and advancement.

A few days passed with no word. In this time, it is now
believed, the necklace went no closer to Marie-Antoinette than
the bottom of the Comte de Lamotte's commodious pocket.
These silent days of waiting by the cardinal were really the lull
before the storm.

Marie-Antoinette is said to have received a letter of cautious
thanks from Monsieur Boehmer. She is also said to have burned
it. But then this is the stage where the real mystery begins to
thicken and perhaps give the lie to the Queen's later disclaimers.

It would seem that Marie-Antoinette certainly knew of the
necklace's being sold by the time the letter from Boehmer and
Bassenge was in ashes.

In that case, why did she say nothing at that time? Of
course, she could have wanted the whole matter to be kept a
secret and not reach the ears of Louis. But if there was nothing
discreditable to be told, why should she come to such a decision?

What follows does not help very much to provide a satisfactory answer to that all-important question.

The time arrived for the cardinal to continue the payments
agreed. He sent the Comtesse de Lamotte to the jewellers, but
the notes she carried were insufficient to placate Monsieur Boeh-

mer, who was suddenly anxious about receiving his money. The necklace was gone.

He wrote to Marie-Antoinette another letter. In it he complained that he was still awaiting the agreed payment.

Marie-Antoinette's reply was couched in terms that left the jeweller stupefied. She not only informed him that she did not have the necklace, but had never ordered it from his firm, either directly or through an intermediary. In a few sharp words she attempted to bow out of the transaction and the mystery to which it had given rise.

But Monsieur Boehmer wanted his money and was prepared to demonstrate as much before the entire Court. It was on Assumption Day, August 15th, almost a year to the day since that clandestine meeting in the Grove of Venus and the handing over of a rose, that he acted, both within his rights and within the law. The Court was assembled for the Cardinal de Rohan to conduct a church service, and the courtiers were awaiting the entrance of Louis and Marie-Antoinette, when, instead of the royal couple, an official flanked by burly attendants entered and arrested the dumbfounded cardinal on a warrant sworn by Monsieur Boehmer.

A few hours later de Rohan was in the Bastille.

The bogus countess was also arrested, and the officers who conducted her to prison to await trial did not overlook Marie Laguay. It would seem that someone had talked to some purpose. There was no point in going to the bogus count's home. He was heading for the coast as fast as horseflesh could convey him. The diamond necklace was still in his pocket.

He arrived in Calais ahead of police agents who took after him; he had a good start, and he reached England safely, still carrying the diamonds. Or so it is thought by most who have studied the mystery of that hectic period following Monsieur Boehmer's drastic action to try to recover what he had lost. For the count is known to have sold some diamonds to a firm of jewellers in Bond Street, London, and received several thousand pounds in exchange. He was not arrested because there was no

extradition treaty between England and France in those less
sophisticated times. The diamonds he sold to Messrs. Grey are
generally believed to have been part of Monsieur Boehmer's
famous necklace. What became of the remaining stones can only
be guessed at.

In France the due processes of the sluggish civil law of those
days finally produced a notable trial before the *parlement* of
Paris in May 1786. One of the most contentious items at that
trial was Marie Laguay's story of impersonating the Queen.
Too many who disliked Marie-Antoinette affected to believe
that the young woman was covering up for the Queen, and that
it was Marie-Antoinette herself who kept that rendezvous with
Cardinal de Rohan in the grounds at Versailles.

Some of the Queen's detractors went further and claimed she
had been pressed for cash and had actually shared in the pro-
ceeds of the sale of the diamonds. But there is nothing save the
word of malignant tongues to support this calumny. The trial,
however, resulted only in damaging Marie-Antoinette's reputation, despite the fact that the judges were careful not to involve
her save as an innocent and damaged party.

What is most likely is that the greedy Lamottes had prised
some of the stones from their settings, and they could have sold
some in France without exciting suspicion. They may have paid
off others in the plot with more of the gems, but among the six
hundred were some large first-water diamonds that have never
been traced. No one knows what became of them, and what
happened to them is part of the remaining mystery.

At the close of the trial the bogus countess, forsaken by her
husband, was sentenced to be whipped, branded on the shoulder
as a thief, and then imprisoned in the grim Salpetrière prison.
Marie Laguay vanished into jail at the same time, and in his
absence the man who had sold diamonds from the world's most
wonderful necklace across a counter in Bond Street was sentenced to serve in the galleys for the remainder of his life.

The Cardinal de Rohan was acquitted by the law, but he was
a man back in disfavour at Court. He was virtually banished to

the abbey of La Chaise-Dieu, where he doubtless found time to reflect on the harsh ways of the everyday world with a prince of the Church.

There are a number of remaining loose threads to this puzzle. First, a new rumour spread throughout Paris that Marie-Antoinette had not only been a party to the trick played on the foolish cardinal, but she had connived with the tricksters in order to ruin him. In short, the whole plot had been a carefully prepared trap. Unsupported, this rumour might have died down within a few months, but the affair was revived rather dramatically when it was reported that Madame de Lamotte had escaped from the Salpetrière prison. She not only escaped, she vanished. This could not have been done without the connivance of someone with power. One did not escape from such a jail without the doors first being opened by those who had the keys.

Not surprisingly, the bogus countess arrived later in London. So did the Duchesse de Polignac, who was known to be a confidante of Marie-Antoinette. Again whispers circulated in both London and Paris, and this particular tale of the two cities was a spicy one. It was to the effect that the duchess had gone to procure from Lamotte a number of letters in Marie-Antoinette's handwriting that he had taken great care did not leave his possession.

This simmering pot of mystery and double-dealing was still bubbling without boiling over when the Paris mob rose and stormed the Bastille. Suddenly Louis and Marie-Antoinette both had something else to think about than an unpaid-for necklace. So had Monsieur Boehmer.

Necklaces and the pale necks that wore them were about to go out of fashion in France. At the time of the notorious trial in May 1786 it did not seem that anything could happen to Marie-Antoinette more terrible than having her reputation dragged through the mire of innuendo and suspicion resulting from the disclosures made at the hearing.

History proved the falsity of such a surmise.

On September 21st, four years after the storming of the Bastille, Louis and his Austrian queen were both imprisoned in the grim Temple prison; and royalty in France was abolished a short while later, when a republic was proclaimed. Marie-Antoinette attended a trial in person and heard herself condemned to death. When in the morning of October 16th, 1793, she mounted the scaffold to be guillotined, only six and a half hours after being sentenced to death, she must have forgotten Monsieur Boehmer's diamond necklace. But history has remembered.

Her name remains irretrievably associated with the mystery surrounding the curious sale and disappearance of that most unlucky piece of magnificent jewellery. The end of the woman for whom it was originally created, the Comtesse Du Barry, was just as tragic. When the torrent of the Revolution engulfed France she was one of the fortunate few who managed to escape out of the country. She reached England, but was tempted to return in the year of the Terror, 1793, to a Paris that had become a charnel house for her kind.

She was denounced and arrested, went through the farce of a trial, and took her place in the tumbril that lumbered its way to the Place Vendôme where Monsieur Sanson's overworked meat-axe awaited her neck.

As a footnote to the horror of those months of the Terror, it may be observed that one principal in the drama of the diamond necklace came through the high tide of revolution without being submerged by it. That was Louis, Prince de Rohan, cardinal of the Roman Catholic Church. He did not die until 1802, having reached an age just two years short of the biblical three score and ten. He too is remembered mainly for the part he played not too intelligently in the mystery of the diamond necklace.

By that time Madame de Lamotte's *Mémoires,* published abroad, had gone out of print. They also achieved a short-lived and dubious success because they charged Marie-Antoinette with complicity in the scandal. But then Madame de Lamotte wanted the book to sell, and she probably felt she had more due to her than a contrived escape from jail and a fast horse to get her out of the country. Besides, she still carried the scars from the whip and the brand of a thief on her shoulder. She for one was destined never to forget the affair of the diamond necklace.

8

The Mystery of the Tichborne Claimant

The circumstances surrounding the trials of the person calling himself Sir Roger Charles Doughty Tichborne make for possibly the most unique historical mystery of the British courts.

The Tichbornes were a wealthy English Catholic family. Their elder son and heir to the baronetcy was Roger, whose mother, a Frenchwoman, gave birth to him in her native land. It was in France that the young boy sat over his lessons before being brought to England and enrolled at Stonyhurst. Later he bought a commission in the army, which he resigned after three years, and at the age of twenty-four he decided to go abroad on his travels.

He crossed to Le Havre, and on March 1st, 1853, sailed in a ship leaving the French port for Valparaiso, in South America. The voyage had only just begun when his father succeeded to the family title on the death of his uncle.

Unaware that he had succeeded his father as heir to the family title, he arrived in South America and after spending a period of some months along the coast of Chile arranged what was an ambitious itinerary for those days. He left Valparaiso and headed inland for Santiago, which was to be his spring-board for crossing the Andes range and continuing clear across the South American continent. He hoped eventually to reach Buenos Aires, and that hope was fulfilled, for in April 1854 he was on the eastern coast of South America. It was on the 20th of that month he stepped aboard a vessel named the *Bella* in the harbour at Rio de Janeiro, and a few hours later she sailed with him from Brazil on a voyage to Jamaica.

Roger Tichborne intended stopping at Kingston, the first stage of his journey home.

However, he did not arrive in the West Indies, nor did the

Bella, for one of her overturned boats was found more than four hundred miles from the nearest land, so it can be reasonably assumed that the ship that left Brazil with Roger Tichborne aboard foundered in a storm.

His family certainly believed that Roger had lost his life in the disaster that overtook the *Bella.* His death was presumed, and in the course of time his younger brother succeeded to the family's title. There was, however, one member of the Tichborne family who refused to believe that Roger had died at sea.

That was his French mother. She clung to the belief that, by some unexplained miracle, he was still alive and would one day return.

So convinced was she that, nine years after he was reported lost with the *Bella,* she demonstrated her faith by having an advertisement for news of him published in *The Times.* Possibly it was little to be wondered at that the other members of the family were not only distressed by this curious single-mindedness, but annoyed, especially the current baronet.

No one answered that first advertisement.

A second, which two years afterwards was printed by various newspapers in Australia, was destined to produce a less negative result—though not in every sense of the word.

The advertisement ran :

"A handsome reward will be given to any person who can furnish such information as will discover the fate of Roger Charles Tichborne. He sailed from the port of Rio de Janeiro on the 20th of April, 1854, in the ship *La Bella,* and has never been heard of since, but a report reached England that a portion of the crew and passengers of a vessel of that name was picked up by a vessel bound to Australia – Melbourne it is believed. It is not known whether the said Roger Charles Tichborne was amongst the drowned or the saved. He would at the present time be thirty-two years of age, is of a delicate constitution, rather tall, with very light brown hair and blue eyes. Mr. Tichborne is the son of Sir James Tichborne, baronet, now deceased, and is heir to all his estates."

That last piece of information was like setting a spark to dry tinder. It not only produced a quick result, but it was one that was terribly destructive.

The Australian advertisement appeared in 1865. As will be seen, it was much more detailed than the London *Times* advertisement, which read :

"If anybody can give any clue of Roger Charles Tichborne and if there are any survivors of *La Bella* they are requested to let Lady Tichborne know of them at 1 Nottingham Place, Regent's Park. A handsome reward is promised for any well-authenticated particulars."

The wording of this advertisement, which appeared in *The Times* of May 14th, 1863, suggests that it could have been drawn up by a solicitor representing Lady Tichborne. If this were indeed the case, it seems a pity that the strong-willed mother of the missing Roger did not consult the same adviser after attending a session with a clairvoyant in Paris, at which she was informed she would see her missing son again. The encouragement she received from highly dubious sources in Paris stimulated the later advertisement in Australia, from which the men of law were to enjoy a most memorable confrontation in the courts.

Not surprisingly it was an Australian solicitor who started the mystery ball rolling. His name was Gibbes, and he lived in Wagga Wagga, New South Wales.

He not only read the advertisement for which Lady Tichborne was responsible, but applied his mind to considering its terms in relation to a client of his, a butcher named Tom Castro. In the course of a conversation with Castro, he remembered, the man had mentioned being shipwrecked and had referred to an inheritance he had passed up in England. He also remembered something else. Castro smoked a pipe. Carved on its stem were three initials.

They were R.C.T.

"What do they stand for?" he had asked.

Castro had laughed, but there was a wry sound to his amusement.

"I just carved them, that's all," he replied, offering no further explanation.

Gibbes called on the butcher, showed him the advertisement in the paper, and challenged his client to say whether or not he was Roger Charles Tichborne. Tom Castro had been apparently reluctant to speak about the matter at all, but the solicitor had been insistent, and at last Castro admitted he was the missing heir.

That, at least, was the tale told later.

In the interim a letter was sent to Lady Tichborne, and its posting was followed by Tom Castro disposing of his butcher's business in Wagga Wagga and taking a ship to England. He lost no time in appearing before Lady Tichborne.

She took one trembling look at him, and cried, "My son!"

She might have chided him for his poor spelling, but then the meeting was calculated to eradicate such a thought from her mind, especially as she had been aware in years long past that spelling, in French or English, was not one of her son's strong features.

The letter that had preceded the arrival of the man from Australia had opened:

"My dear Mother,

The delay which has taken place since my last letter dated April 22nd, 1854, makes it very difficult to commence this letter. I deeply regret the trouble and anxiety I must have caused you by not writing before."

It had referred to the solicitor in Wagga Wagga in these terms:

"Mr. Gibbes suggested to me as essential that I should recall to your memory things which can only be known to you or me to convince you of my Identity. Namely the brown mark on my side and the card case at Brighton."

But it made no mention of an incredible drama that had been played through in Sydney, before the butcher from Wagga

Wagga caught the ship to bring him to England. He was not alone when he arrived in Sydney. His wife and child were with him. He installed himself in a comfortable hotel and began to run up a sizable account with the greatest ease. Two former servants of the Tichborne household were in Sydney at the time. One was a former gardener named Guilfoyle, the other a West Indian named Bogle who had for a time been a valet. Each accepted Tom Castro as the missing Roger Tichborne without reserve. Possibly for this reason the man now calling himself Tichborne was afforded the credit on which he called so substantially.

When presented with his formidable hotel bill he had not the cash to settle it. But completely undaunted he wrote out a cheque for ten thousand pounds, to buy the hotel, and he formally engaged the hotel manager's son as a private secretary at a salary of five hundred pounds a year, a very handsome sum in those days.

The one snag about such an arrangement was that the cheque was drawn on a London bank at which Roger Tichborne had no account and never had one. That, however, was to be learned at what might be truthfully termed long last.

The man who was to become famous as the Tichborne Claimant landed in England with something of an entourage. As well as his wife and child, who were accompanied by a nurse-maid, he had brought the West Indian valet and Bogle's small son. The party from Sydney arrived to learn that Lady Tichborne was in Paris. When he crossed the Channel to see her he apparently did not deem it necessary to take with him the pair who would have been her daughter-in-law and grandchild. Instead he travelled with a brewery salesman he had first met in a billiard room and a lawyer this man had introduced him to and whom he had asked to represent him.

The meeting in Paris was sealed with a kiss, the smiling mother calling on the man she considered her son, for he claimed he was too ill to forsake his bed. As she lifted her head from kissing him and announcing he was indeed her son, Lady

Tichborne murmured, "Ah, he looks like his father." She shook her head hesitatingly for a moment before adding, "His ears are a little like his uncle's."

The lawyer so conveniently acquired by the man from Down Under needed no further words from Lady Tichborne to be prompted into declaring that she had identified her son. It seemed a detail hardly worth pointing out at the time that Lady Tichborne's eyes were failing. Cataracts were forming over them. She probably saw the man in bed in Paris more clearly through her wishful thoughts than through her clouded vision.

Somewhat surprisingly the alleged Roger Tichborne recovered from his bed of sickness with dramatic speed after Lady Tichborne's triumph of faith. He did not linger in France, but hurried back to England to rejoin his wife and small daughter and to lay claim to the Tichborne title and estates. It was as though Tom Castro, who had been content to jog along carving carcases and separating offal from the more highly priced joints of meat, was suddenly a person of different outlook, pretensions, and claims.

Moreover, he was a man in a hurry. While he might be prepared to put the due processes of law in motion, he gave no sign of being happy to rely upon their sluggish advance. He began seeking persons who could accept him as the missing Roger Tichborne and would further his successful bid as the rightful claimant to the family's fortune.

So began a bewildering and bedevilling series of acts which, in the long run, served only to emphasize the mystery surrounding the person and claims of this Tichborne claimant from the other side of the world. While the new claimant began cutting a deep furrow through the social divisions of the London of his day, the Tichborne family mustered their reserves and set about providing formidable opposition to the newcomer, whom they declared an impostor.

The division of opinion spread. Not only the members of the Tichborne family and those to whom the claimant introduced himself took sides in the controversy, but the ordinary man and

woman in the streets began to decide for themselves whether the
claimant was false or genuine.

The claimant was seemingly as cavalier in the matter of
paying his London debts as he had been in paying those he had
incurred in Sydney. But in London he could not stall those who
dunned him for cash, nor could he forestall writs by signing
cheques on fictitious bank accounts – not if he wished to stay
out of jail, and that was something he desired very devoutly. He
had too much to perform and accomplish while enjoying his
social freedom.

To this end he secured the services of two redoubtable members of the Bar, the brilliant Serjeant Ballantine, and Dr.
Edward Kenealy, Q.C., both men of considerable experience in
dealing with charlatans and mountebanks. However, not before
the loquacious tradesmen of London had had their client declared a bankrupt. They received this information with a grim
determination to reverse the trend of their client's sad fortunes.
For they not only believed his story of being the genuine Sir
Roger Tichborne, but they believed in him, the man. Perhaps
it can be argued that they had to, for by the time the case was
ready to come to court there was a second claimant to confuse
the overall issue.

Roger's younger brother, who had succeeded to the title on
the death of their father, Sir James Tichborne, had died and
left a widow and a son he had sired but not lived to welcome
into this stormy world for Tichbornes. Alfred's widow was
anxious to have his posthumous son established as the family
heir.

By the time the first examination was held which would clear
the way for a jury trial of the claims brought by one-time Tom
Castro that individual had changed out of all recognition. He
was no longer lean, but girdled with several stone of solid fat.
Some said he had a glandular disease, others that his only
disease was his gourmet's appetite. But he cut a curious figure,
with his coat buttoned to breaking point across a chest over
which a moon face decorated with mutton-chop whiskers

brooded. He gripped his silk hat in one hand, his gloves in the other, and proceeded with a knock-kneed gait, his chubby legs straddling over his out-turned feet.

He appeared at the inquiry and explained that he had adopted the name Castro because he had known a Tomas Castro at Melipilla, a place he claimed to have passed through on his earlier trip from Valparaiso to Santiago. The solicitor, Mr. Holmes, appearing for the strangely changed lean and tall young man of the early fifties, counselled writing to Melipilla. This was done. Back came replies recalling an English teenager named Arthur Orton, who in no way fitted the picture of a wealthy Englishman of later years.

Mr. Holmes could not but feel that enthusiasm had swept him from his best course when he digested the unhelpful news from South America. The unfortunate man became subject to acute legal indigestion when, some time later, the Tichborne family lawyers sent out their own agent to Melipilla to make inquiries on the spot. From this exercise in uncovering the past they were directed to a family of East End butchers named Orton, a young member of which, named Arthur, had years before gone to South America.

To the Tichborne family and those who supported them against the tubby claimant it was plain enough that young Orton had continued his wandering progression from one continent to the next and had finally arrived in Australia, where he had fallen back on the skills he had learned in his youth in the family's butcher-shop in Wapping.

However, to those who managed to remain impartial while the pros and cons were squabbled over, it became clear with the lapse of time while the case continued before the courts that there was every likelihood that while the claimant was not Roger Tichborne, he was also not Arthur Orton from Wapping. A conclusion that added profoundly to the degree of mystery enveloping the claims being aired at great length before an interested general public.

One person who was spared the ordeal of the trial that

opened on May 11th, 1871, was the purblind but doting Dowager Lady Tichborne, whose health succumbed quite suddenly to the March winds of three years before, and she died on the 12th of that blustery and chilly month.

It was a particularly chilly month for the pudgy man she had accepted as her long-lost son. He was without the impact her testimony might provide at the trial.

Fruitlessly he worked to fill the swift gap in his forces. In the event he found that nothing could make up for what he had lost.

The trial duly opened under the unequivocal gaze of the presiding judge, the Chief Justice of the Common Pleas, Sir William Bovill. Opposing Serjeant Ballantine, who led for the claimant, was the Tichborne family's leading counsel, Sir John Coleridge. He was the Solicitor-General.

Various persons who had known Roger Tichborne in the past were brought forward to be questioned and for their answers to go on the record. Brother officers in the Sixth Dragoon Guards and the Carabineers said they recognized in the claimant the young officer who had served with them nearly twenty years before. A military tailor named Greenwood supported the claim that the man he had recently met after a long lapse of years was the Roger Tichborne for whom he had made uniforms in the past. When asked about the claimant's trousers, however, he replied, "Within half an inch the same. That's only the length, of course. He was so much stouter than when I saw him first – considerably stouter – the only thing left about him is his eyes."

At that Sir John Coleridge had smiled with a show of pleasure. For earlier he had cross-examined Major-General Custance, who had known Roger Tichborne in Ireland, on what the witness had meant when he referred to the returned Roger Tichborne having a peculiar expression about the eyes.

"What was the nature of the expression?" he had asked.

"I cannot explain," the witness had replied.

"Cannot you give us a notion?" urged the Solicitor-General.

"No, I cannot explain it, though I am perfectly aware of it."

"Did you ever see anyone without an expression in the eye?" the witness had been pressed.

"I think everybody has an expression in the eye," he had admitted, "more or less."

"But can you give us any idea at all what you mean by this peculiar expression about the eye?"

"No."

That had ended the attempt to obtain a more contentious description. But now another witness was referring to the eyes of the man who was calling himself Roger Tichborne. Those eyes beamed with seeming benignity when Anthony Biddulph, a Sussex J.P. who was cousin to Roger Tichborne, said, "My deliberate judgment is that he is my cousin. The more I see of him the more I am convinced he is my cousin."

However, under Sir John Coleridge's cross-examination this amiable witness for the plaintiff admitted knowing the West Indian named Bogle and had it dragged from him that Bogle could have known a good many facts about the Tichbornes that would have proved full of valuable information to anyone to whom he imparted them. But it was rather like drawing teeth. For example, when asked if Bogle could have known about some unique pipes Roger Tichborne had possessed in his earlier life Anthony Biddulph contented himself with the one cautious word, "Possibly."

The Solicitor-General asked him, "Would you oblige me by going as far as 'probably'?"

"Probably, perhaps."

"Will you say 'probably' without 'perhaps'?"

"Probably, then."

By which time the Sussex J.P. was looking as though he had had more teeth drawn than he felt he could afford to lose for comfort.

A long, dragging procession of witnesses filed into the court and climbed into the witness box, day after day, all bent on cudgelling memories which the other side were bent upon proving were faulty. Friends, relatives, teachers, tradesmen, they trod

on one another's heels, said their piece, and answered questions
with, sometimes, a sort of inverted humour, like the laundress,
Martha Legg, who had been to the altar with a husband more
than once.

She was asked, "From your conversation with him, what is
your opinion?"

"That he is Sir Roger," she replied spiritedly. "No other
person could have said to me what Sir Roger said when I first
came into the room."

"What did he say?"

"He said, 'You've the same face as ever. You're the woman
who had an old man for a husband'."

"Is it a fact that your first husband was an old man?" she
was asked.

"Yes," she said with no hesitation. "He was thirty years older
than me."

As the trial continued and the procession of those ready and
willing to play their part in the drama steadily lengthened, it
became apparent that the public was applying its own means of
simplifying the issues involved, to make them not only more
understandable, but more easily acceptable, according to the
point of view one favoured.

Serjeant Ballantine and Dr. Kenealy were champions endeavouring to return a man of honour to his rightful place in
society, as wished by his dead mother. One could cry over the
picture if one had the tears to spare.

Or one could incline to the alternative viewpoint, and see Sir
John Coleridge as a defender of the rights of a widowed mother
and her small son whose inheritance, so justly his, would be
snatched from him if this stranger from Australia succeeded and
won the case.

The persons to be impressed, of course, were those silent
individuals who sat through the hours-long wrangles and argu-
ments and debates with a look of quiet suffering on their faces,
unable to get up and leave the jury-box when they became
bored by the interminable proceedings, which went on for

months. That jury which sat for the hearing of the Tichborne case in 1871 was no ordinary one. It was designated special.

This meant that the members sitting on the panel of jury men were qualified to take their seats by reason of their owning substantial property. They were deemed the appropriate kind of citizen to make up their minds about what was essentially a claim against property. Their foreman was a grave-faced Welshman who was one of a band of compatriots who were grafting their ideas and plans for large drapery emporiums on the British capital. Their influence is still felt today, a century later. The jury's foreman was named Henry Dickins. His drapery store was the one run under the name of Dickins and Jones.

He and his fellow-jurors must have frowned intensely at an incident that occurred shortly after Sir John Coleridge asked the claimant his mother's name.

"Henrietta Felicité," he replied.

Or, rather, that is what he thought he said. But he pronounced the second name Feleceet. From somewhere in the well of the court the voice of an unknown who had been offended by such a display of ignorance corrected him.

"Felicité."

A most incredible error to be perpetrated by a young man who, if he was what he claimed to be, had spoken only French up to the time he was sixteen. When he refused to describe the quadrangle at Stonyhurst, or even to say how many sides a triangle had, Sir John Coleridge seemed to have the plaintiff on the defensive. Enough to be jabbed into a retort that brought a laugh in court. This came after the claimant had been asked, in reference to his schooldays, what chemistry was about.

"It's about chemistry, of course," he retorted.

"Yes, I know," nodded his questioner. "History is about history and Greek is about Greek. What is chemistry concerned with?"

"Chemistry is different herbs and different poisons, mixture of medicines."

"Things you get in a chemist's shop?"

"I think a dose of it would do you good."

But when the involuntary laugh had subsided it was the leader for the defence who was smiling. He could afford the light laugh at his expense, for the cost had been well incurred. It was painfully obvious to everyone listening that the stout man in the witness box had only a limited notion of what the word meant to a student of chemistry – as Roger Tichborne had been at Stonyhurst. This kind of painfully dragging charade became too much for the jury when evidence was produced that, while a child in Brittany, Roger Tichborne had been tattooed by a French sailor with an anchor, a cross, and a heart, yet the claimant did not have such a tattoo mark on his body. By this time more than sixty witnesses had been called for the claimant. The family's defence promised a hundred witnesses.

The prospect was frightening to serious-minded business men of the kind who made up the jury. The foreman glanced around at the others sitting with him after the business about the non-existent tattoo marks had been finally closed, and received a few sharp nods of encouragement. Whereupon he rose and had everyone in court looking at him as he informed the Bench, "We have heard enough. We wish to find for the defendants."

So the famous case closed with the suddenness of a draught blowing shut an open door. But all was not over for the Tichborne Claimant. Sir William Bovill, the presiding judge, had the erstwhile plaintiff committed for trial on a charge of criminal perjury. No bail was allowed. This meant that the flabbergasted plaintiff had within a few minutes become a prisoner pending his trial at the Central Criminal Court.

The second trial was another wrangle. Basically the issue became a question of whether Tom Castro was Arthur Orton. Few thought of him any longer as Roger Tichborne. But the prisoner refused to admit he was Arthur Orton, despite the pressure put on him by the prosecution. The criminal trial lasted even longer than the civil action, a hundred and eighty-eight days. The two trials had lasted through two hundred and ninety days by the time Lord Cockburn had summed up and the jury had found Castro guilty.

Lord Cockburn addressed him in the following terms :

"Thomas Castro, otherwise called Arthur Orton, otherwise called Roger Charles Doughty Tichborne, baronet, after a trial of unexampled duration you have been convicted of the several perjuries charged in the counts of this indictment."

He continued to the moment for sentencing the prisoner, when he said :

"The sentence of the court which I now pronounce is that, for the perjury alleged in the first count of this indictment upon which you have been convicted, you be kept in penal servitude for the term of seven years; and that for the perjury alleged in the second count of this indictment, of which you have also been convicted, you be kept in penal servitude for the further term of seven years, to commence immediately upon the expiration of the term of penal servitude assigned to you in respect of your conviction upon the first count of the indictment, and that is the sentence of the court."

In such ponderous words the prisoner was sentenced to fourteen years' penal servitude, and he was taken to complete ten of them and be released from jail in 1884. It was said he was as ready as ever to press his claim to the Tichborne fortune and title. But he was without funds and almost without friends, so it is not surprising that in 1898 he died and was buried in a pauper's grave without having effectively given another challenge to those who had defeated him. Yet the family that had spurned his claim curiously allowed on his coffin, provided free by a sympathetic Paddington undertaker, the words : "Sir Roger Charles Doughty Tichborne."

Why, if the claimant had in truth been an impostor?

Dr. Kenealy, one of his counsel during the memorable trial, had no doubt that the claimant was the genuine Tichborne he professed to be. He continued to further his client's lost cause long after prison gates had closed on him. It has been observed that, so strongly did Dr. Kenealy feel Castro to be the genuine

Roger Tichborne, he continued to speak up on his behalf for years afterwards and at one time even ran the risk of being disbarred for his loyalty to an unfortunate client.

Castro's identity has never satisfactorily been explained, but one thing is certain; this man who arrived in Britain and proceeded to wrap himself in layers of mystery, so far as the courts and general public were concerned, would never have arrived had he not been shown an advertisement in an Australian newspaper. The Dowager Lady Tichborne refused to believe she would not see her lost son again. At least she died before the scales could be cruelly ripped from her weak eyes. Or, if they had been, would she still have claimed Castro as her son?

9

The Mystery of King Sebastian

For a person from what is often termed an ordinary walk of life to vanish with no warning provides no exceptional mystery, though it is possible that the circumstances surrounding such a disappearance might well prove puzzling in the extreme. After all, men and women have been vanishing unaccountably from the beginnings of recorded history, and possibly before then.

On the other hand, for a crowned king to disappear without leaving a trace of his passing or a clue to where he had departed is wellnigh without precedent. But in circumstances as curious as the man's own personality at least one king contrived to do such a thing, with disastrous results for a great many of his subjects.

Why he vanished, how he went, and if he was induced to return in even stranger circumstances are questions still awaiting answers after the lapse of five hundred years. Legends have grown up, not very surprisingly, about this mysteriously vanished monarch, and even in what might well have been his own lifetime the wildest rumours circulated in south-west Europe about his return in the guise–of all choices!–of a pastrycook.

Today the history books usually give a date for his death and the one most often selected is 1578. In that year Francis Drake had been away from Plymouth for a twelvemonth on his famous voyage around the world.

It was an age when valiant deeds were in the making and valiant men had a mind to cross oceans and subdue heathen lands. Although he was neither an explorer nor a navigator, King Sebastian of Portugal was a man of his time. He believed life was to be lived – but as he wished to live it. He desired conquests – if he could bring them about. In fact, he wanted so many things that some of them seemed to be contradictory as achievements. Not that this deterred Sebastian, who strove at the same time to be something of an ascetic and also a man of parts, sophisticated for the times in which he lived.

Sebastian was young, and his curious code of personal behaviour resulted in a mysticism that was baffling to his friends and well-wishers and seemed at times quite fanatical in the enthusiasms it produced. But he was yet another king in Europe who came to the throne at an age too young to understand what ruling a nation of men and women living ordinary lives really meant or implied for their ruler.

Sebastian became King of Portugal at the age of three.

He was born in 1554 and was his country's monarch in 1557, on the death of his grandfather, John III of Portugal. He was descended from that same John of Gaunt who had helped the claims of Henry Tudor in the previous century.

While he was a child the business of ruling the country was taken over by his grandmother, Queen Catherine, and his great-uncle the cardinal, Prince Henry. These joint regents kept all matters of State from interfering with the boy's upbringing, which was left to the Jesuits.

It was these scholars of the Church who were responsible for so directing the youngster's studies that they fired him with a holy zeal to lead his own crusade against the hosts of Islam, the avowed enemies of Christians in any holy war, and dangerous neighbours in southern Europe and the lands bordering the Mediterranean.

Sebastian's minority ended in 1568, when he was fourteen. He was then deemed a king capable of ruling in his own right. But for Sebastian his new-found freedom from restriction meant only one thing.

Now he could prepare to lead his crusade. The time had come when he could demonstrate what kind of warrior king he could be to his people.

He considered where he would take his armies when they were ready, and after studying a map of Africa felt drawn towards the challenge of that north-western area where the followers of the Prophet had established a régime in what is now Morocco. He felt that if he launched an expedition against that region and cleared it of Moslems he would not only be striking a blow for his faith, in the manner of the Crusaders of earlier times, but would be extending the boundaries and influence of Europe, and of Portugal in particular.

This last could have been especially a challenge to him, for his neighbour on the landward side in Europe was the powerful and threatening Philip II of Spain, who had ascended his own throne the year after Sebastian was born; so that Sebastian could be said to be living in the shadow of the King of Spain, and he had not the temperament as a young man to live out of the sun. The shadow cast by another man did not appeal to him as a place to reside, though he was perhaps to learn differently.

This is part of the mystery still surrounding Sebastian and what actually became of this king with curious notions about kingship.

To forward his dream of empire – which, he confided to his close friends, envisioned a Portuguese colony in Africa crossing that continent from the Atlantic to the Red Sea – he surrendered the functions of a ruler to the Jesuits who had been his mentors and were responsible for his upbringing. It was a Jesuit axiom that, if they were given the child to educate, they would produce the man they desired. They may have deemed they had reason to consider Sebastian was, in some ways at least, the exception that proved their rule.

It is to be doubted that the Jesuits in Portugal wished Sebastian to become the dreamer of action he proved himself to be unless it was their intention to get their own hands on the power that stemmed from the crown. If that were indeed the case, one has to view the Sebastian they created in the light of subsequent events. With Sebastian gone, Philip of Spain was able to move in, with a nominal blessing from the Pope in Rome, and rule Portugal, making the country a subservient vassal of Spain. In this connection it is well to ponder that there were many more Jesuits in Spain than in Portugal, and the Order is one that brooks no indiscipline. Moreover, those were the days when

what was, to modern ears, oddly termed the Holy Inquisition
was breaking bodies and burning live flesh in an extremely
fundamental way of destroying heresy – by destroying the her-
etic through fear and pain.

Yet the influence of such beliefs can be seen to have made
Sebastian want to do just that – destroy the Infidel who did not
share his faith. Furthermore, when one considers the choice for
such a campaign open to Sebastian, one can see that he had
very little. Philip's armies were sprawled like a steel stain across
the Low Countries, where Protestants were being massacred.
The same fate was reserved for Elizabeth's England if Philip's
troops could ever land in sufficient strength to beat the opposition they encountered in that misty island off the European
mainland.

Sebastian may have wanted to prove something to Philip by
his crusade. He certainly was driven to try to prove something
to himself. We cannot be sure whether he was successful in
offering proof to himself and are even less sure about whether
he returned to plague a King of Spain who had thought little
enough of him and had swept up his kingdom into the Spanish
empire as though it were a pile of leaves in Vallombrosa in the
fall of the year.

Sebastian had grown out of his teens with his dreams of
leading a crusade. In those years he had led a strenuous life,
preparing himself for the hazards of conquest overseas. He spent
long hours in the chase and was a fearless hunter in the saddle
or on foot. He was adept with military arms, and was an
opponent in the field of skill and courage, a hard man for any
enemy to defeat in hand-to-hand combat. To complete his
fitness for his chosen life he underwent periods when he lived an
ascetic existence, denying himself all fleshy pleasures. By the
time he was twenty he was a very unusual young man, but he
was ready to lead his first armies to North Africa.

Those were days when armies moved with ponderous slow-
ness, and the expedition to Morocco undertaken in 1574 by
Sebastian did not prove to be a conquering sweep of Moslem

enemies either into the sea or into the burning sands of the
Sahara. Sebastian's Portuguese army did not get very far from
the shore, and little more can be claimed for the expedition than
that it arrived and returned later. The interval between was not
productive of valiant feats of arms or awe-inspiring military
exploits. In any practical sense Sebastian was able to achieve
little except gain a scanty first-hand knowledge of the terrain
over which he proposed to fight later, for that was suddenly his
intention. To return at a later date, better equipped, with larger
forces, and capable of striking a more resolute blow for his faith.

The Portuguese army went back to its ships, which headed
north for the River Tagus, and Sebastian started preparing for
his return. His second host left Portugal four years after the
first. This time he found the Moors ready for him. It was as
though they had expected his return and had been waiting.
Sebastian was not given an opportunity to fling his new army at
the enemy. The enemy struck first.

It was dawn on August 4th, 1578, when the Moors, with
their throat-aching shouts to Allah and their curved swords
brandished aloft in the newly risen sun, hurled themselves on
the Portuguese army and caught Sebastian's men by surprise.
The place where the two armies met was known to the Moors
as Al Kasr al Kebir. The Portuguese invaders wrote the place-
name as Alcazarquivir. The similarity is easily recognizable.

The battle was one of fury and great blood-shed, with the
Christian banner of the Cross often within a short crossbow shot
of the green flag of Islam with its sweeping Crescent. Leading
the Moslems, and striving to reach Sebastian to engage him in
personal encounter, was the warlike sovereign emir of Fez. So
determined were the leaders to cancel each other out that their
personal rivalry helped the later stages of the battle to become
confused.

Of the little that is known it is difficult to say where fact ends
and legend begins.

However, the slaughter of the Portuguese was great, and it
has been generally assumed that Sebastian was one of those who

died on the field of battle. The assumption, however, has been attacked fairly strenuously, and the attacks began while the battlefield was still littered with the bodies of the slain.

Luiz de Brito was one of the Portuguese taken prisoner after the Moslems had routed their foes. He is responsible for the story that, when all seemed lost, a close friend of King Sebastian's urged him to escape.

"You have done all you can. What remains to be gained?" the friend cried.

"Heaven," Sebastian is reported to have shouted above the clash of arms, "if we deserve it by our deeds," and again turned towards the swarthy faces of the enemy who were hewing down his men.

Luiz de Brito said that it was some time later that he was able to wrap the royal standard of the House of Braganza around his own body and follow Sebastian's slim boyish figure towards a river that ran some distance from the rear of the Portuguese position, but he was intercepted by pursuers because the banner's folds slowed his progress. His last sight of Sebastian was of the young king running towards the river's bank.

Much later it was learned by those who made enquiries that among a band of Portuguese fugitives who reached Arzilla, where Sebastian's ships rode at anchor, was a figure muffled in a wide cloak. This person was shown great deference by the others who followed him aboard one of the ships. But his face was not seen, and all that could be ascertained of his build was that it was slender.

The ship weighed anchor with the other vessels and headed for Portugal with the remnants of the defeated army.

Legend has superimposed on this slender evidence the story that the young King Sebastian had taken his crushing defeat as a humiliating blow and had decided he could not face his people at that time as their ruler. He had reached Portugal in secret and had immediately made preparations for a personal pilgrimage to the Holy Land. He eventually set out with only one or two personal attendants, without having let his people know the truth.

Now comes a gap. He is supposed to have sent back to Portugal a number of letters, and it is true that the State archives contain letters of this period that might have been in his handwriting, but of this there can be no certainty. Some letters did arrive from Palestine bearing a sign manual said to be his, but again there is plenty of room for doubt about authenticity. Yet these papers do contain various statements sworn by pilgrims returned from Palestine who claimed to have seen him in the Holy Land. According to such testimony, he had retired to a cave not far from Damascus and was living the harsh life of a religious anchorite. This would at least have been consistent with his former outlook and fanatical convictions during his period of asceticism. But at that time there were many such religious hermits in the Holy Land, and returned pilgrims could have been genuinely mistaken in believing they saw the young king living a life of penance and devotion away from the company of his fellows.

What is more positive, as proof of sorts, is the ring brought back from that part of the world by a pilgrim who claimed it had been entrusted to him by a man he was able to recognize as the vanished king. He had been asked to take it to Lisbon and give it to some relatives of Sebastian's who lived in the city. The ring is kept with the State archives. It has been identified as Sebastian's. But whether Sebastian was the person who gave it to a returning pilgrim cannot be certain. At least, however, it would seem possible.

For that to be the case the body buried by Sebastian's victorious foes at Al Kasr al Kebir had to be someone else's. It was later removed and taken to Ceuta, on the coast, a spot some sixteen miles from Gibraltar's Rock.

Philip of Spain was sufficiently interested in learning that the body believed to be Sebastian's had been interred in North Africa to petition Pope Gregory XIII to proclaim formally that Sebastian was dead and Portugal was without a king. Philip was a ruler on whom the Pope in Rome was leaning rather heavily at that time. The proclamation was provided in due course, and with it Philip found he had good and sufficient reason to usurp the vacant throne near the Tagus. In 1580, two years after the disastrous crusade to North Africa, Philip annexed Portugal. The Portuguese weren't happy at being taken over without their feelings being considered, but in time they found his rule of increasing benefit, for, whatever else he was, Philip was a king who believed in wearing his crown, sitting on his throne, and being seen to rule in the way he believed a king should.

Two years after annexing Portugal Philip annexed the body in the grave at Ceuta, which he believed was Sebastian's. He had the body brought across the Mediterranean to Lisbon, where, with due pomp and ceremony, it was interred again, this time in the Convento dos Jeronymos.

Perhaps he thought to make this resting-place a shrine. If so, he was disappointed. But he did manage to satisfy a great many of Sebastian's subjects that he had brought their last Portuguese king home to rest among them, and that was a gesture which was appreciated.

Of course, at the same time, it established that Sebastian was dead and accepted as dead by the new king and by the Pope. That should have ended, in Philip's view, any lingering doubt as to whether Sebastian had survived the battle.

Instead, the scheming Philip was plagued with a veritable rash of pretenders, all claiming to be Sebastian, who had survived the battle and gone his secret way, suddenly to decide it was high time to change his mind and put in another royal appearance.

Two of these came to be known from their birthplaces. One was the King of Penamacor and the other the King of Ericeira. There can be no reasonable doubt that they were fakes, for they were shown to be the children of peasant families in those two places. Their kingly titles were proffered derisively. But for a time each made himself a nuisance with his claims and railings against the Spanish forces in the country. They were rounded up within a year of each other, the first in 1584, the second in the following year.

If they had done little else, these untutored pretenders had given expression to the growing rumour that Sebastian was still alive and would return.

The third of the pretenders appeared later, but was a more formidable proposition for the authorities under the Spanish crown to deal with. He appeared at a time when what has been called Sebastianism was growing throughout Portugal. Indeed, this belief in the eventual reappearance of the country's manly young warrior king came to form its own mysticism and through various changes of national climate was equated with a return at a time of national need.

In a curious way the values of the legend that was growing up about the king who would return became, in many instances, a latter-day equivalent of many of the mystical beliefs that formed the Arthurian legend of the Celtic races.

The greatest threat to Philip came from the man who suddenly appeared in Valladolid and said he was Gabriel Espinosa, a pastrycook. It is said, however, that he was an indifferent maker of pastry, but was always well dressed and had his pockets well lined. Moreover, his linen was invariably freshly laundered, a sign in those times of a man being of gentle blood.

Why he came to Valladolid no one ever discovered, but he rented a house and acquired a housekeeper who thought a great deal of her own appearance. She became possessive towards her employer, and when he tired of her ways they quarrelled and he told her to pack her things and leave.

In a spirit of vengefulness she called on the local head of the city's gendarmerie, and did her best to make trouble for the man who called himself a pastrycook.

"He's no pastrycook," she declared. "He is someone of high birth who has a secret to hide. With my own eyes I have seen the jewels he keeps locked away. They are worth a king's ransom."

They were certainly the right choice of words to interest the police official she had visited. But his interest penetrated a little more deeply than the spiteful woman had allowed for. First he had her confined so that she could not spread this story to other ears. Then he called at the house where Espinosa lived. He found it empty.

It appeared that the man who called himself a pastrycook had suddenly decided on flight. The police official accepted this as a challenge. He summoned his men and began to visit every inn and tavern in the vicinity. Midnight came and went with the tired men in bedraggled uniforms tramping into darkened inn-yards and rousing the landlords.

At two in the morning they came to a small *posada* that was actually beyond the city's limits, and this time they heard of a traveller who had arrived late. When shown to the man's room Gabriel Espinosa was found asleep in bed.

The room was shabby as one would expect, but beside the bed were bags filled with gold coins and gold-mounted pieces of personal property, such as a drinking-cup made of rhinoceros horn. Among this strange traveller's belongings was a prayer-book with heavy goldwork on its covers, which were also gem-encrusted.

However, inside this unusual possession was an inscription in a fine hand, which proclaimed the prayer-book to be a gift from the Princess Isabella, King Philip's daughter, to her cousin, Donna Anna.

With the coins was a collection of diamonds, and after pawing over his find the police official was awed to come upon a miniature portrait of no less a person than King Philip. It had been engraved on a solid gold plate. There was a similar engraving of Donna Anna, which was set in diamonds.

Treating the man he had roused with a mixture of respect and resentment, the police official asked Espinosa to give a satisfactory account of how he came by such possessions. The reply of the man he had awakened surprised and baffled the questioner.

"I am," said the man still sitting on the bed, "a pastrycook. I have a business here in Valladolid and another eight miles away, in Madrigal. The jewels you see are the property of the Princess Anna, King Philip's niece, who is a nun in the convent at Madrigal, and she has entrusted them to me to sell."

Only an investigation could prove or disprove such a strange claim. The police official resorted to further questions, and learned that Espinosa had left his house because the house-keeper was a slut.

"Why should you care?" Espinosa was asked bluntly.

"Because I am a pastrycook," he retorted. "I cannot abide dirt and sluttish ways."

The police official decided he had to search the clothes worn by a mere pastrycook, and motioned to a couple of his gaping gendarmes to go through the pockets of the clothes draped over a wooden chair.

"Take care," Espinosa suddenly called sharply. "Remember that I have the power to punish and the power to reward." He added something even more puzzling. "If need be I shall exercise my full rights."

The police official wanted proof that he was dealing with a thief and would not be intimidated. It was when the lining of Espinosa's rich doublet was searched that four letters were found. Before the first could be read Espinosa snatched them from the hand of the police official and stuffed the sheets into his mouth. He was given no time to swallow them, but was knocked down and tied hand and foot. At this Espinosa's anger spilled over.

"I'll have you broken on the wheel for this," he threatened. Again he added an odd expression for a pastrycook. "It is the person of your king you are dishonouring."

Such fine words did not loosen the bonds binding the self-professed pastrycook's limbs. He had to lie fuming while the police official scrutinized the contents of the letters taken from his doublet. Two were from the vicar-general of the convent at Madrigal, and the others were from Donna Anna, who was abbess of the convent. Both wrote in terms of great respect and addressed the person to whom the letters were sent as His Majesty, Dom Sebastian, King of Portugal, and the terms of the abbess's letters were suggestive of her being personally attached to her correspondent.

It was an unhappy tangle for a police official to have to sort out, and the official at Valladolid quickly realized that this was a procedure best avoided.

Accordingly he had the pastrycook removed to the city's prison and held against his return, while he set off for Madrid. In the Spanish capital he sought audience with Philip, and not before receiving some rebuffs from Court dignitaries at length found himself closeted with the Spanish king out of earshot of his guard.

His story and the proof he brought to support what he told the king shocked that short-tempered monarch, who had a simple way of acquiring the truth – torturing those whom he thought were concealing it from him. The vicar-general at Madrigal was secretly seized and put to torture. It may be that it was this treatment of a churchman that turned some of the Spanish Court against Philip in his hounding the persons he considered involved in another plot with a fresh pretender for the throne of Sebastian. However, he procured little of real satisfaction from the unhappy priest, and even less from Gabriel Espinosa, who received a similar brutal treatment. All that can be said about Espinosa after he was passed to Philip's torturers is that his boast of having the Valladolid police official broken on the wheel was never made good. He is said to have maintained that he was the returned Sebastian, whereupon the torture continued to make him admit he was lying and to name others in the plot. Espinosa did not retract his claim.

It was the vicar-general who finally made a show of confessing. He said the pastrycook was indeed Sebastian. Pressed upon the point, he amended this by saying he and Donna Anna believed the pastrycook was Sebastian and added that the money was to regain his throne.

That was bad enough for Philip. There was worse. The vicar-general rubbed salt in a very raw wound by continuing to confess to having solemnized at Madrigal a marriage between Donna Anna and Gabriel Espinosa. He went on to say there had been a child of this strange union inside the convent, a little girl, who had been put in the care of two nuns. The child's guardians had been sworn to secrecy. The marriage had been arranged in order that there should be an heir to the Portuguese throne.

Naturally, true or false, this story spelled out in Philip's ears the grim word treason. Those were days when clandestine liaisons and secret marriages were undertaken for reasons of high policy. Only a few years before the involved story of Mary Queen of Scots had ended with an execution for what amounted to treason in the same vein. Philip had no mind to be lenient. He believed Espinosa was an impostor who had deluded a kinswoman of his. When he made other inquiries it was to learn that Espinosa had supporters in both the Spanish and Austrian Courts and among some of the Jesuits. The only reason for giving him support was because his story of being Sebastian returned from a Middle Eastern pilgrimage was believed.

The vicar-general at Madrigal was sentenced to death and hanged in Madrid.

Gabriel Espinosa was also sentenced to death. His execution took place in Valladolid, where it would make less of a stir than in the larger city. Others who were alleged to have been in a plot to present Espinosa in due course as Sebastian were arrested, tried, and also hanged.

The gullible Donna Anna, as she seemed in Philip's stern gaze, was imprisoned for life and her child vanished, presumably to be brought up with no knowledge of the curious mixture of blood flowing in her young veins.

So far as Philip was concerned this mystery of the self-proclaimed pastrycook ended on the gallows at Valladolid in 1594. He himself died four years later, a man who had seen his most promising dreams turn to veritable nightmares and one who had learned an uncomfortable lesson, that the pleasure one can derive from mere power is brittle and liable to crumble as one savours it.

But that almost indefinable belief in Sebastianism had not died with the pastrycook of Valladolid, despite his persistent claim to be the vanished king.

Five years after Philip's death another pretender to the vacant throne appeared, one who, rather astoundingly, could speak no word of Portuguese. He made his appearance rather dramatically in Venice in 1603. He told a story that was convincing enough for many to believe him, and he rallied supporters to his cause.

However, his claim to being the Sebastian who had been in Morocco a quarter of a century before seemed noticeably less shiny and stainless when it was learned that his name was Marco Tullio, and that he hailed from Calabria in the toe of Italy.

Unquestionably there was little mystery about him. He was a gambler who put his life in the balance and lost his gamble. As a loser his life was forfeit, and it was taken very promptly. Like the previous three pretenders he died on the scaffold.

But his brief passage across the stage of history served a purpose he probably was not aware of himself. It kept Sebastianism, as a creed, alive in Portugal. Supporters of the creed were members of that strange and rather loose political faction who believed in the quality of Portuguese nationalism as expressed by the hopes of those calling themselves Sebastianists. They were active plotters and insurrectionists during the early years of the seventeenth century. When the big crunch came, and the challenge was finally thrown out to the occupying Spanish forces by the Portuguese, Sebastianists provided not only many who took an active part in the rebellion, but also a number of the planners who decided how best to make the effort to wring their independence from Spain.

That was in 1640.

By then the Sebastian legend had become a mystical part of

belief in the ability of Portugal, one of Europe's former colonizing Powers, to rise again to the great heights of the past.

It was too late for any death-defying Sebastian to return if he had not already done so, but by this time the man was no longer important. Only the legend mattered. Perhaps that was what Luiz de Brito really wrapped around his waist and handed on to future generations on that fateful August morning when the Crescent triumphed over the Cross.

10

Mystery of the Lost Dauphin

A little more than two months following the taking of the Bastille by the Paris mob a banquet was held in the main salon at Versailles. It was to celebrate the arrival of the Flanders Regiment to reinforce the National Guard units under the command of the Comte d'Estaing. It was a festive occasion despite the fact that France was on the point of supplanting a monarchy with a republic. Louis had been troubled by the realization of how close he and his family remained to Paris, the seat of the most militant revolutionaries, and pondering how he could get his family to Metz and possibly even across the frontier out of a land that seemed to him bent upon its own wanton destruction.

But there had been no opportunity to leave Versailles, and bringing the Flanders Regiment to reinforce the garrison troops seemed the best move to ensure the safety of his wife and family and their personal staff. There was disquieting news from the town of Versailles, where revolutionary fervour had expressed itself by the plundering of a baker's shop and the beating of the baker for the crime of baking two qualities of bread.

On the night of September 23rd, 1789, however, Louis was of a mind to enjoy himself among officers who commanded loyal troops. After the visitors had eaten their repast and drunk the loyal toasts with shouts of acclaim the royal family appeared among them and joined the festivities. While Louis the proud father looked on, Marie-Antoinette led her small son the Dauphin down the long hall past the tables crowded with enthusiastic diners in bright uniforms.

Little Louis, hailed as Monsieur le Dauphin, was four, a curly-haired boy with bright eyes and flushed cheeks. The picture presented by him holding his mother's hand and walking among the gathering of fighting men was remembered years later in his memoirs by Joseph Weber, Marie-Antoinette's foster-brother, who was at Versailles that night.

He wrote: "At the sight of so much majesty and grace, of so much beauty and innocence, sentiment and admiration reached the height of intoxication, and all eyes were filled with tears of emotion as the music intoned the touching air of *Richard Coeur-de-Lion*:

> 'O Richard! O mon roi!
> L'univers t'abandonne.'

"This air, which made such a striking allusion to the situation of Louis the Sixteenth, and which for so long a time has been proscribed in France, was repeated in chorus by all lips. Never had there been a more loyal concert. Never had a purer sentiment stirred a whole assembly. The august faces of the king and queen bore that evening the imprint of contentment and happiness, instead of the melancholy of several months past."

It was the last occasion the ill-starred family were to know when they could smile with pride and pleasure. Days later the mob stormed to the doors of the royal apartments, and were only held off by a tired-out Lafayette, who didn't seem very sure of his militia or himself, and when finally the royal family started back to Paris under guard the little Dauphin was crying because he was hungry.

His hunger that grey rainy day was to be the least of the boy's miseries.

Just over a year later Louis, virtually a prisoner in the Tuileries palace, with some six hundred National Guard as eager jailers, stood at a window and decided he must escape with his family. He told Marie-Antoinette he had made up his mind. Former plans to escape in the previous March, travelling by way of Compiègne to Brussels, had been called off because of last-minute hitches. There had been another scheme prepared in the following October, but that too had been abandoned. Now Louis was thinking again of reaching Metz, the place of refuge that had been in his mind when he had first thought of trying to escape from Versailles.

"I shall write a letter to Monsieur Bouillé," Louis told the queen. "I shall not leave France. To make for Belgium or England does not attract me. In France I can perhaps mediate and bring peace."

Marie-Antoinette, Austrian-born, thought of her children, the Dauphin, now five, and his sister, known in Court circles as Madame Royale, and said wistfully, "We should be safer outside France."

"But I am the King of France," Louis reminded her gently.

In the event the argument about whether to remain in France or not after they had escaped proved merely academic. There was to be no escape. But an attempt to escape was made.

Plans were laid in February 1791 by the Marquis de Bouillé, a cousin of Lafayette and lieutenant-general of Louis's armies. He was in command of the troops in the east of France, and had put down an insurrection in Nancy, the chief city of Lorraine. In his reminiscences he later recorded: "I had made the necessary arrangements and preparations for the departure of the king, which was to have taken place during the first days of May. Everything had been arranged at Montmédy for his reception and for the assembling of a small body of troops under the cannon of that fortress, at a mile's distance from the country of Luxembourg."

So that, should the revolutionaries pursue Louis to Montmédy, there would be a good chance of overcoming the king's scruples about leaving France and getting him and his family over the Luxembourg frontier into safety.

But the secret departure was held up until midsummer, the loss of another six weeks, so that when the flight was attempted it was on one of the shortest nights of the year. The royal party was led through a door where no sentry was posted to a waiting carriage. The coachman holding the reins was the Comte de Ferson. Madame de Tourzel, the royal children's governess, was acting the part of the owner of the carriage. The king was to be

her valet and the queen her maid, in case the party was stopped
and questioned.

The inconspicuous carriage rumbled away from the Tuileries
and made for the western outskirts of the sleeping city. By five
o'clock in the afternoon the dust-covered brown coach was
bouncing its wheels over the stones of Châlons and the noble
coachman unhurriedly continued beyond the town and headed
for Sainte-Menehould, which he reached about half-past eight,
when there was still a great deal of light in the sky. An hour
and a half later the coach had caught up another, bearing
others of the royal party, at Clermont, and the fugitives turned
north towards the village of Varennes-en-Argonne.

At that time Louis had no suspicion that a revolutionary
named Jean-Baptiste Drouet had recognized him from his
likeness on a banknote. That had been at the gates of Sainte-
Menehould. A detachment of dragoons, ostensibly to ensure the
safe passage of treasure in a coach, had been held up by members of the National Guard that had been roused by the active
Drouet, who had then with some mounted companions given
chase. In Clermont Drouet had heard of the coaches that turned
north. He caught them up in the tiny village street of Varennes.

The royal party's passports were demanded, and they surrendered those procured by the Russian Ambassador for the enter-
prise. The name of the coach's owner was given as the Baronne
de Korff. She was said to be on her way back to Sweden. The
party were shown into the house of a man named Sauce, and
the Dauphin and his sister were set down on a bed to go to sleep
while the adults wrangled.

It was by this time nearly midnight. Louis suddenly wearied
of pretence as he listened to the sounds of a crowd collecting in
the streets outside, and admitted he was the king.

At that moment he was barely twenty-five miles from the
army under the command of the Marquis de Bouillé. Had he
not stopped for more than half an hour on the hillroad before
entering Varennes the royal party might have escaped. But in a
letter detailing final arrangements de Bouillé had written "The

relay will be at Varennes," but had not named the inn where the fresh horses would be waiting for the royal party. Had the name of the inn been known to the royal party the coach would have gone straight there, the change of horses would have been made, and the royal party might well have been too far on the road to Malmédy to be stopped by Drouet and his companions on tired horses.

The inn where the horses waited for the royal party was the Grand Monarque. It is still in the village today. The omission of the inn's name from that letter, plus the sharp sight of Jean-Baptiste Drouet, possibly changed the course of French history, perhaps even European.

The royal party was escorted under guard back to Paris and temporary imprisonment in the Tuileries, where Madame Campan, the lady-in-waiting to Marie-Antoinette, was shocked to see that her royal mistress's hair had turned white.

Only months were to elapse before the attack on the Tuileries and the slaughter of the loyal Swiss Guards wrote one of the most terrible pages in the story of the French Revolution, but afterwards the monarchy was doomed. The royal family became prisoners in harsh fact as well as in spirit. They were removed to the grim Temple prison, and all Europe awaited the outcome, knowing that Louis would be put on trial for his life.

This was begun on December 11th, 1792. He was arraigned in the name of Louis Capet. His death was decreed, and on a bitterly cold day in the following January he was drawn to the guillotine erected in what was then known as the Place Louis XV.

So died Louis XVI, or Louis Capet as his jailers had called him.

Behind him in the Temple prison he left another Louis Capet, a little boy who was to be taken from the care of his mother, herself to be guillotined before the year was out in the name of the Widow Capet.

She lived long enough to suffer seeing her son the Dauphin of France coarsened into an insensitive ragamuffin clothed in vile-smelling rags. The change was wrought in a surprisingly short time from a bright, intelligent child of captivating manners. He was the rightful heir of the Bourbons and to large numbers of French their king, Louis XVII. But to the depraved and brutal custodians of the inmates of the Temple prison he was not even called Louis. They preferred to refer to him as Charles Capet. Perhaps Louis was too vivid a reminder of the boy's executed father.

The Committee of Public Safety, the body with the real power since France had changed from monarchy to republic, looked upon the boy as a menace to the safety of the State. He was eight years old.

One of its spokesmen, Jacques-René Hébert, voiced what the menace implied when he said, "In the minds of both royalists and moderates the king never dies. He is in the Temple. If they could seize this phantom they would rally round him."

In the Temple prison with the Dauphin was his sister. In a moment of pique, wanting the children out of Paris yet not sure where to remove them, Hébert told a friend, "Let this little serpent and his sister be cast on a desert island. I do not know any reasonable means of getting rid of them, and yet we must rid ourselves of them at any price."

Very possibly he was recalling the words of the forceful Deputy Réal, who had announced, "Louis is not to be feared any more, but do you count his son – that interesting child who is supported by an ancient prejudice – as nothing? Believe me, he is an hostage who must be carefully retained."

The Louis Capet in the Temple prison, then, was at eight years of age the focus point for a great deal of revolutionary concern and even hate just for being born the son of his father.

Hébert, in an uncharacteristic moment of sentimental truth, had called the boy "as beautiful as the day", but of course he did not stipulate which particular day he was alluding to. His colleague Chaumette, who described himself as "National Agent", whatever that was meant to imply, and certainly made it his business to control the treatment meted out to the prisoners in the Temple prison, did not indulge in sentiment of any kind.

"The young whelp," he maintained cynically, "must lose the recollection of his royalty."

It was on such advice that the decision was taken to remove the boy from the company of his sister and mother. The removal of the son from his mother's charge was undertaken at a late hour with no warning.

Louis was awakened from sleep when the door of his room was banged open in the middle of the night and a lantern's light shone in his squinting eyes. He sat up on his cot and saw his mother on her knees, pleading with municipal officers wearing their broad tricolour sashes of office. He heard her words as she begged them in the name of God to leave her son with her.

Then he saw his sister, who was fifteen, push forward and plead with his mother. Madame Royale remembered the grim scene when she penned her recollections of those tragic years.

"At last," she wrote, "Mother consented to give up her son. We got him up, and after he was dressed Mother surrendered him to the municipal representatives, while bathing him with tears, as though she foresaw that she would never see him again. The poor little fellow embraced us all most tenderly, and, weeping, departed with the men."

That was the moment when the mystery of the lost Dauphin really started. The little boy who had been presented to the officers of the Flanders Regiment at Versailles, who had been smuggled out of the Tuileries palace and borne on his mother's lap along the bumpy road to Varennes, who had upon another occasion cried with hunger when driven from Versailles to Paris, and who had been terribly frightened that day when the mob had committed obscenities with the bodies of the Swiss Guards, walked into the night with the men wearing gaudy waist sashes and what became of him is subject for speculation and surmise.

The revolutionaries claimed he died and his family later

accepted the fact. But others have insisted that he was not allowed to become a victim of the Terror and of the rule of Robespierre, that seagreen incorruptible according to Carlyle, but it was a seagreen tinge that often looked a muddy brown when viewed through a scarlet haze of fresh-spilled blood.

The known facts are few. Perhaps most pertinent of all is that the boy was handed over to the care of a brutal and degenerate ex-cobbler named Simon.

The boy's new jailer was an unprepossessing man, whose appearance was calculated to scare a child torn from his mother in the middle of the night. But the very pattern of that memorable separation was to set the seal on what was intended for the child's future.

Simon was chosen because he was brutishly stupid and totally uneducated. He was told to root out any aristocratic ideas with which Charles Capet might have been imbued. Simon was the man to delight in such a piece of human destruction. He went to his task with the will of a dedicated disciple of Chaumette and Robespierre, who had authorized the boy being given into his charge.

Part of his personal system of character destruction was to teach a delicately nurtured boy the foul language of street blackguards and back-alley cut-throats. Madame Royale tells us :

"Every day we heard him singing revolutionary songs and other horrors with Simon. He made him sing them at the windows in order to be heard by the guard, with terrible oaths against God, his family, and the aristocracy."

It was a process of education, and it was rendered intensively, to obtain the most rapid permanent results. As it proved, Simon was an excellent choice of teacher, within weeks turning the shy and politely brought up young king into a cringeing guttersnipe with a cesspool for his mind.

Perhaps no one is better entitled to picture the change in the boy king than his sister :

"Louis XVII had been imprisoned in the part of the Tower

that had been occupied by the king. There the young prince, called the wolf cub of the Temple by some of the regicides, was abandoned to the brutalities of Simon, former shoemaker, drunkard, gambler, and debaucher. Innocence, youth, and misfortune; the angelic face, weakness, and the tears of the royal child – all were without power to soften the ferocious guardian. One day, when he was drunk, he nearly knocked out an eye of the young prince who, by a refinement of cruelty, was compelled to serve him at table. He beat him without pity.

"One day, in an access of rage, he held an andiron over his head and threatened to beat him to death. The descendant of many kings was constantly exposed to coarse expressions and obscene songs.

" 'Capet,' Simon said to him one day, 'if these Vendéens rescue you, what will you do?'

" 'I will pardon you,' replied the young king."

It is a poignant picture, but it is of the stuff of legend. It is very much to be doubted if the boy was ever reminded that he was a king in his own right, despite the creation of a republic. His mother had been so insistent on demanding news of him that, to solve a growing problem, she was removed to the notorious Conciergerie, where she remained confined in an increasing atmosphere of degradation until the October morning she was taken out to be introduced to his guillotine by Citizen Sanson, who personally roused her from sleep punctually at seven.

What is pertinent is that Simon only continued in charge of his young prisoner for three months after the execution of his mother. On January 19th, 1794, Simon was relieved of his post and was no longer responsible for the custody of Louis Capet. His place was taken by four special commissioners appointed by the Committee of Public Safety, and from the time they took over the known history of Louis XVII ceases.

In the Temple prison his name was not mentioned. His aunt and his sister were still kept in the prison, but neither heard his voice calling out in pain or shrieking obscenities any more. The doctor who at intervals had called to examine him ceased his visits.

A rumour sprang up around the neighbourhood.

Charles Louis Capet, it said, had been removed to a noisome damp cell where he existed in solitary confinement throughout each day, his only companions being the rats who invaded his dark quarters to fight for his meagre ration of food. There is something blood-chilling about that picture if one dwells on it and its implications.

Robespierre, at the height of his power, had a plan which included the lost Dauphin. It was to make the little king a kind of undeclared hostage in negotiations with the European Powers who were then at war against France and the extreme revolutionaries who were running the country.

In furtherance of his plan he considered removing the small captive from the underground cell in the Temple prison to Meudon, outside Paris to the west. What is known is that a British secret agent reported in London : "On May 23rd Robespierre went to the Temple prison to fetch the king and take him to Meudon."

A later report from the same British secret agent stated : "The king was brought back to the Temple on May 30th."

The very natural question that arises here is—was it Louis Capet who was returned to the Temple prison? If it wasn't, then who was the boy imprisoned in his stead, and why was the exchange made?

At that time the man in command of the troops in Paris was the titled revolutionary, the Comte de Barras, who had been out in the streets the day Camille Desmoulins told the mob to attack the Bastille, and who had taken part in the attack on the Tuileries which virtually ended the monarchy.

He left his own story after seeing the revolution out and Napoleon's new empire in, but unfortunately he was a notorious liar, especially as an author. However, it is known that he visited the Temple prison out of interest after Robespierre's visits. He had the young captive called Charles Capet shown to him, and saw a stupid-faced child with a bloated body and puffy hands who in no wise resembled the remembered picture he had of the Dauphin. When he left the prison he returned to his office and appointed a fawning underling named Laurent to be sole custodian of the royal children. A change took place in the living conditions of the prisoner called Charles Capet. When Laurent became responsible for him the boy was no longer in a damp cell, as rumour had earlier maintained. He was kept close confined, but in an apartment away from other prisoners. Servants who maintained the fire in the room and attended to cleaning and dusting were not allowed to see the prisoner. They only knew the room was occupied, supposedly by the boy who was Louis XVII.

A few months later, on December 19th, 1794, three delegates from the Committee of Public Safety visited the Temple prison ostensibly to report on "the state of the services".

Their names were Citizens Harmand, Reverchon, and Mathieu. They were shown into a well-lighted room that was kept clean and where a boy of about nine years of age sat at a table building castles with playing cards. The three delegates stood inside the door staring at him in silence.

He lifted his gaze and stared back with complete lack of interest. His features remained fixed in a blank expression, and he said nothing.

However, the delegation had a job to do and on which they would have to prepare a report. They tried to get the boy to talk to them. They tried for three hours, and then gave up a hopeless task. He had not said so much as yes or no in answer to the scores of questions they had patiently put to him.

When they left they were perturbed. The Terror was over. Its chief architect, Maximilien-Marie-Isidore Robespierre, had been arrested by a gendarme of nineteen named Méda on July 28th and guillotined in his turn the next day. Times were changing enough for the delegation that left the Temple prison to wonder whether continuous ill-usage had reduced a once bright and vivacious child, known to be talkative, to a state of speechless idiocy.

They made their report, but such was its tone that the committee who received it decided it should not be made public. Nothing was done as a sequel to the handing in of the secret report so far as can be discovered.

In that case the boy prisoner might have continued building his castles with playing cards for another six months. He had no visitors save the prison staff and the only unexpected visits he received were from a doctor, who usually frowned when he examined the apathetic youngster. On June 6th following that December visit from the delegation of three from the Committee of Public Safety the little prisoner in the Temple prison was suddenly too sick to rise from his bed. The doctor was summoned.

He shook his head again, prescribed medicine, and went away. He came the next day, but saw nothing in the prisoner's room to lift his frown.

For two days the boy remained ill in bed. At three o'clock on June 8th, 1795, he gave a tremulous little shudder and died.

A post-mortem examination was held on the small body, which was then placed in a cheap white-wood coffin and borne away at nine o'clock at night to a common grave known locally as "the trench" in the churchyard of Sainte-Marguerite.

His sister recorded the occasion in these words:

"During the winter my brother had several attacks of fever; he was always near the fire. He had several deplorable crises. Fever set in, he grew constantly weaker, and expired in agony. Thus on June 8th, 1795, at three o'clock in the afternoon, died Louis XVII, aged ten years and two months."

She has something to say about his last illness:

"I do not believe he was poisoned, as was said at the time, and as it is still rumoured. The falsity of this is borne out by the testimony of the doctors who opened his body; they found no traces of poison. The only poison which shortened his days was the bad sanitation added to horrible treatment, cruelty, and unparalleled harshness."

With the small body in the white-wood coffin were buried the hopes of French royalists and supporters of the Bourbon cause – but only for a time.

Rumours were soon circulating that the boy who had been buried had been poisoned because he was a liability to a changing régime. Other rumours maintained that the boy was not Louis XVII. It was argued that the differences between the Dauphin and the bloated boy seen after Robespierre's visits were too marked for them to be one and the same youngster. Then what had happened to the real Dauphin if another boy had been substituted for him?

Rumour supplied the answer to that question also.

Simon had, despite himself and his crude brutalities, grown attached to his young charge. So the story went when more fanciful versions of what had taken place in that room of mystery in the Temple prison were circulating not only in Paris, but throughout France and Europe.

Angry at being dismissed from his post, the boy's jailer had smuggled him out of the Temple prison when he left for the last time.

But the rumours did not say where Simon had taken the boy or point to what had become of him. However, they were sufficiently strong to encourage pretenders to come forth and raise the hopes of French royalists waiting for their own miracle to change history.

In fact, there was a constant stream of such pretenders to the throne of the Bourbons. They numbered thirty in all, each insisting he was the lost Dauphin returned to claim his own as the rightful Louis XVII. Not that Madame Royale wavered in her own belief of what had happened to her brother and why. She left it to the historians of a following century to theorize about the fate of the little boy known to his revolutionary jailers as Charles Capet. Some wild theories have been advanced, but none has replaced the accepted date of Louis XVII's death, June 8th, 1795.

On the other hand, the element of doubt and mystery has never been completely removed, so that the tragic figure of the small prisoner in the Temple prison remains a challenge to all who try to find how much truth lies in the maze of surmise, or if, indeed, there is any truth at all in it.

What is a possibility not usually considered is that the child of delicate health succumbed before 1795. He had suffered considerable hardship at the hands of Simon, both physical and mental, and there is no reason to suppose that those who followed the brutal ex-cobbler were any more lenient with a sickly charge. It could be that mental and physical deterioration had been so great that the boy died in spite of last-minute efforts to save his life.

This would be the opposite of the theory that he was poisoned.

He would have to be replaced, in that case, because at the time of the Meudon journey he was a pawn on a political chessboard. But in that case it would have been another boy who was taken to Meudon and brought back, a journey undertaken to show Europe the son of Louis XVI was still alive. It would not have been the first time such a deception had been practised by hard-pressed politicians.

This could have happened inasmuch as there is nothing to disprove it except the records by men who were known to be anxious to have a story told that explained their prisoner's not being available to be shown.

But, lacking proof, all is surmise after the brutish Simon picked up his few personal effects and walked out of the boy's life—if he did.

Whatever the truth concerning the lost Dauphin, history has made its own adjustment, and in the tables of Bourbon kings Louis XVII is shown to have been nominal King of France from 1793, the year his father was executed, until 1795, when the body of the boy from the Temple prison was buried in its cheap coffin of unvarnished wood.

But Louis XVIII is not shown to have become king until the year Napoleon abdicated, 1814. For a period of nineteen years the Bourbons did not recognize a king save that lost Dauphin whose bones were possibly mouldering with those of others interred in "the trench" of Sainte-Marguerite. When at last the brother of Louis XVI, the Comte de Provence, assumed the title of Louis XVIII the story of little Louis Capet, the lost Dauphin, was finally closed.

The boy's uncle issued his first proclamation as king in resounding terms. It began like a clarion call: "The impenetrable decree of Providence, in calling us to the throne, has created a striking similarity between the beginning of our reign and that of Henry IV, as though it desired to indicate that this great king is to be our model. We will imitate his noble frankness." After some challenging references to the past quarter of a century it added: "No, we have no doubts. Soon the cry of 'Long live the King!' will succeed seditious clamours, and our faithful soldiers will gather around the throne, fighting for its defence, and reading in our paternal regard forgetfulness for the past."

But all that too was only a dream.

The bright sun of the Bourbons was setting behind a deepening mist that night Marie-Antoinette saw her small son taken from his cot by the hard-faced men with tricolour sashes and handed over to the inhuman Simon.

The Bourbons who clung to the throne of France from 1814 until another tide of revolution swept them into the gutters of history in 1848 were men trying to make terms with the past and finding it impossible to achieve.

Men looked at them and averted their gaze. Too often they saw the pathetic picture history has given the world of a little boy whose last tragic months were cloaked in a mystery that is all the more pathetic because it cannot be solved beyond the last doubt.

Julie Smith
Dene House
Fairway.